M
DISCIPLES
IN THE TWENTY- FIRST
CENTURYCHURCH

How the Cell-Based Church
Shapes Followers of Jesus

JOEL COMISKEY, PH.D.

CCS Publishing
www.joelcomiskeygroup.com

Published by CCS Publishing
23890 Brittlebush Circle
Moreno Valley, CA 92557 USA
1-888-511-9995

Cover design and Layout by Sarah Comiskey
Editing by Scott Boren

LCCN: 2013931465
ISBN: 978-1-935789-42-0

All Scripture quotations, unless otherwise indicated, are from the Holy Bible, New International Version, Copyright ©1973, 1978, 1984 by International Bible Society. Used by permission.

CCS Publishing is the book-publishing division of Joel Comiskey Group, a resource and coaching ministry dedicated to equipping leaders for cell-based ministry.

Find us on the World Wide Web at **www.joelcomiskeygroup.com**

PRAISES FOR
Making Disciples in the Twenty-First Century Church

I've read all of Joel Comiskey's books, but *Making Disciples in the Twenty-First Century Church* is his best work yet. In this book Joel reminds us that the real call and challenge of the Church is not developing leaders or numerical growth, but "making disciples who make disciples." He also helps us understand why that is best done in a cell or small group context, and gives us great insight about how to make that happen. I'm looking forward to having all of our Pastors, Coaches, and Cell Leaders and Members read this book in the near future.

—**Dennis Watson,** Lead Pastor, Celebration Church of New Orleans

I am so excited about Joel Comiskey's new book, *Making Disciples in the Twenty-First Century Church*. When

I'm asked what makes a cell church thrive, I always say, "discipleship." Thank you, Joel, for unpacking discipleship; not just as an endeavor for individuals, but as the critical element for creating a church community and culture that reproduces the Kingdom of God all over the earth. I pray this book won't only be read, but lived out as we were made to make disciples.

—Jimmy Seibert, Senior Pastor, Antioch Community Church President and Founder, Antioch Ministries International

I really like that Joel asked the *Why* question before the How question. He even takes on the What question which is just as important. The interest in discipleship is greater now than anytime in the last fifty years. I fear however that we are using the same words but are not speaking the same language. I recommend this work, I cheer Joel on, he joins many of us who are masters of the obvious. It seems so obvious that our purpose is to be disciples and make disciples. I cheer him on because he goes beyond the What and Why and does address the How. This will help any person who reads it and I pray that there will be many.

—Bill Hull, Author of *Jesus Christ Disciple Maker, Disciple Making Pastor, Disciple Making Church,* and *The Complete Book of Discipleship,* Adjunct Faculty at Talbot School of Theology, Biola University

The history of the cell church movement in Brazil has many names of great man of God. Joel Comiskey certainly is one of them.

We see how over the years his understanding of the New Testament Church has deepened. Again Joel surprises us with this jewel.

He covers many aspects of cell church life, showing us how discipleship relates to the broader scope of it, and how to shape followers of Jesus. He takes us to the heart of the matter of the cell church as he states it:

"The purpose of cell ministry is making disciples who make disciples."

Excellent book. The movement in Brazil, certainly, will be blessed through this book. Enjoy it.

—Robert Lay, Cell Church Ministry in Brazil. Pioneer in the cell movement in Brazil, and publisher of Joel's books

In his tremendously helpful new book, *Making Disciples in the Twenty-First Century Church*, Joel Comiskey cuts directly to the core purpose of cell ministry, which is "making disciples who make disciples." Then he tells us how to do it through the Cell-Based Church. Like Joel's other books *Making Disciples in the Twenty-First Century Church* is solidly biblical, highly practical, wonderfully accessible and is grounded in Joel's vast research and experience.

Great job Joel!

—Dave Earley, Lead Pastor, Grace City Church of Las Vegas, Nevada Author, *Eight Habits of Highly Effective Small Group Leaders* Adjunct Professor, Liberty Baptist Theological Seminary

For more than twenty years Joel Comiskey has served the cell church movement. He has helped scores of congregations move from being traditional churches to communities where edification and harvest occurs. *Twenty years!*

Now he combines two decades of observation as his capacity as a researcher. He has scoured many books to assemble wise counsel for us. His discussion of how community varies from culture to culture is indeed penetrating. As I read through the pages I mentally noted specific Christian workers who need to read these pages.

Thanks, Joel, for the way you allow the King to speak through you to enlarge His Kingdom on earth!

—Ralph Neighbour, Jr, key pioneer of the cell church movement.

Joel Comiskey continues to deepen our understanding of the cell-based church. In Making Disciples we are equipped to carry out the Great Commission at maximum capacity. Get ready to have your vision for ministry strengthened and expanded!

—Andrew S. Mason, Small Groups Pastor, Thrive Church, Elk Grove, CA. Founder, *SmallGroupChurches.com*

As one of the world's leading experts on cell-based churches, Joel Comiskey is well placed to show how New Testament-style disciple making works. His decades of experience in fields of ministry all over the world confirm that every-member ministry and personal investment in disciples are God's pathway to true maturity and expansion of the kingdom of God. This well-written book deserves attention from every serious Christian!

—Dennis McCallum, Author, *Organic Discipleship*

TABLE OF CONTENTS

DEDICATION

To the Joel Comiskey Group board (Steve
Cordle, Rob Campbell, Mario Vega, Jeff Tunnell,
and Celyce Comiskey), who have supported,
guided, and blessed my ministry and writing for
the last twelve years.

ACKNOWLEDGMENTS

I'm grateful for the help I received in writing this book. My name is on the cover, but without the expert eyes of the following people, many errors would appear on the pages.

Anne White labored for many hours to find and correct numerous errors in this book. I first met Anne during my Ph.D. days at Fuller Seminary, where she was editing doctoral degrees for students like myself. I'm grateful for her friendship and volunteer help in perfecting this book, including many of the finer details (e.g., footnotes, capitalization, and so forth).

Jay Stanwood, a retired engineer and good friend of mine for about thirty-six years, helped order my thinking by suggesting new phrases and correcting some biblical flaws. Jay has a way of taking my complicated statements and suggesting simpler, more concise phrases.

Bill Joukhadar, a fellow cell sojourner-- www.cells-church. com now living in Australia, discovered errors no one else had found and then offered wise counsel to correct those mistakes. Thanks mate.

John and Mary Reith offered loads of encouragement, along with a few corrections. Both love to read and inspired new confidence in me.

I appreciated Patricia Barrett's work in looking at this book. She both critiqued and complimented my writing.

Rae Holt has been a long-term supporter of Joel Comiskey Group, and I'm very grateful that he takes the time each year to offer his critique and suggestions for my books.

My good friends and team members on the JCG board, Rob Campbell and Steve Cordle, looked over the manuscript to make sure I was on the right track, and I appreciate their counsel and friendship.

Scott Boren, my chief editor, pressed hard to help me stay focused on discipleship in this book. At various times I wanted to buck his advice and write more generally on cell church, but I'm so glad I listened to his consistent advice to stay focused on the main theme. Scott's editing skills has made this book so much better.

Lastly, I want to thank my wonderful wife, Celyce, for being my best friend and providing the liberty and encouragement to write this book.

INTRODUCTION

I've been helping churches develop healthy cell groups since 1994. Along the way, I've realized that the service I provide these churches is heavily influenced by my own convictions about cell ministry. In the past, for example, when I primarily focused on faster church growth through cells, my training and coaching didn't build a strong foundation. I noticed how frequently pastors and churches left cell ministry to pursue another program or technique when cell ministry didn't produce immediate growth.

I realized I had to dig deeper to understand the *why* of cell ministry in order to help churches over the long haul. My search to find answers took me back to Christ's commission to make disciples who make disciples (Matthew 28:18-20). I now believe that making disciples is the proper motivation for implementing the cell strategy (or any ministry). Christ-like disciples are formed within the cell and the cell system (equipping, coaching, and holding larger celebration gatherings).

When a pastor grasps the vision to make disciples who make disciples, a new, purer motivation compels the church forward because of a better understanding of the why of cell ministry. Understanding that the cell strategy is primarily about making disciples who make disciples rescues cell ministry from superficial techniques and showy statistics. It places cell ministry squarely within a biblical model for ministry. As I help pastors to stop focusing on outward models and to understand why they are doing cell ministry, I feel like I've succeeded.

A number of books have been written about cell church ministry. Many of those books are general and try to cover everything about cell ministry in one book.[1] My goal in this book is to focus on one thing: the purpose of cell ministry, which is making disciples who make disciples. I will cover many aspects of the cell church but my goal is to explain one thing: how those different parts point to the goal of shaping followers of Jesus.

Part 1

WHY CELLS?
WHY DISCIPLESHIP?

Chapter One

WHY WE DO
WHAT WE DO?

Simon Sinek, popular speaker and author, was considered a "successful" businessman. Even though he was making a lot of money, he lost his passion and motivation for doing business. Sinek, like so many, began to focus on what he was selling and then trying to figure out *how* to sell it. Yet, he realized he was missing *why* he was selling the product. Sinek began to study great innovators, leaders, and companies who started with the *why* question. These great companies and people inspired those who worked for them with ideals and vision because they knew their purpose.

Through the struggles to rediscover excitement about life and work, Sinek made some profound personal discoveries and began helping his friends and their friends to find their *why*. He eventually wrote the bestselling book, *Start with Why*, to teach how to go beyond superficial motivations for life, business, or ministry.

He noticed that companies that started with *what* or *how* often resorted to manipulative techniques to sell their products, promoting the short-term benefits. Sinek says, "Addicted to the short-term results, business today has largely become a series of quick fixes added one after another after another. The short-term tactics have become so sophisticated that an entire economy has developed to service the manipulations, equipped with statistics and quasi-science." [2]

He realized that just because something works doesn't make it right. In fact, the danger of manipulation is that it might work so well that a company or a person begins to depend on wrong tactics. Many scams, Ponzi schemes, and dictators depend on wrong motivations and tactics to achieve amazing results—but are eventually exposed over time.

Sinek's principle is very simple: start with the *why* question and know the true motivation that should guide the company or organization. After spending lots of time meditating and working out the *why* question, the *what* and *how* question will naturally follow. [3] He says, "By *why* I mean what is your purpose, cause or belief? *Why* does your company exist? *Why* do you get out of bed every morning? And *why* should anyone care?" [4]

Most churches know *what* they do and how to do it. Yet few truly understand *why* they do what they do. If the pastor can't clearly articulate *why* the church exists, members have a hard time following. To truly inspire a church, the pastor or leader needs to embrace and articulate a compelling, God-honoring vision.

THE PRIORITY OF A PROPER MOTIVATION

In the early days of my cell journey, I focused more on the *how* and the *what* questions. I wrote about *how* cells could grow churches. While it's important to know *how* to do cell ministry, I've learned that the most important consideration is the *why* behind doing it. If the motivation is faulty, leaders become discouraged over time, lose the joy and excitement of leading or supervising cell groups, and often quit all together. If the motivation is only *how* or *what*, the vision will soon dry up and fizzle.

When a pastor or leader doesn't fully understand why he is implementing cell ministry, he can fall into the trap of following someone else's model or thinking a new technique will produce growth. Faulty motivations, however, produce superficial results. Correct motivations sustain over the long haul and give meaning and purpose to *what* we do.

Answering the *why* question also gives the leader added flexibility. He or she is not bound to a particular methodology or result. Rather, the leader is free to adjust, adapt, and create the necessary structures and strategies to succeed over the long haul.

I've lived and practiced cell church ministry both in North and South America. I've also studied many worldwide cell churches and conducted seminars in these churches. I've become increasingly aware that *how-to* formulas usually only work effectively in particular cultures and receptive environments. The formulas rarely transfer across borders and cultures. Those who succeed in cell ministry learn to dig beneath the *how-to* question and unearth the why motivation. The *why* question provides the vision or driving force behind cell ministry and allows the leader to keep pressing on in spite of the obstacles.

In fact, the *how* question often locks a church into certain patterns that probably don't fit the exact circumstance where the church is located. Only answering the *how* question leaves the pastor and church looking for formulas from someone else's model and feeling frustrated when those techniques don't work.

In contrast, fully answering the *why* question gives longevity to cell ministry because the pastor realizes that cell ministry flows from a solid biblical base. When a leader grasps the *why* question, the *how* question flows naturally. In fact, the leader discovers that there are many ways to do cell ministry and one size does not fit all. The pastor can steadfastly plod through the valleys because of a firm conviction that the church is on the right path.

We as believers know that the Bible is our guide book and that scriptural teaching must guide all we do and say. But is there a guiding theme in scripture, one that stands out above the others? Before examining eternal guiding principles for your ministry, let's look at some pitfalls that need to be avoided.

THE INADEQUACY OF SUNDAY ATTENDANCE GROWTH

Many pastors and leaders are motivated by increased attendance growth in the larger worship services. They've been influenced by the discipline of *church growth*, a collection of teachings first formulated and promoted by Donald McGavran in the '70s and '80s and popularized by Peter Wagner in the '80s and '90s. Is there anything wrong with wanting more people in the Sunday worship services? No. But is church attendance growth an adequate motivation for a pastor or leader?

I think of my friend, Pastor John. His church was firmly based on a biblical philosophy for doing ministry, yet he suddenly switched gears after coming back from a miracle conference held in a church that had seen incredible growth through their *miracle strategy*. Pastor John wanted more people attending his church, so he abandoned his previous philosophy of ministry and started following this new church growth model. Pastor John was motivated by attendance growth.

The emphasis on more people in the larger worship service creates problems such as:

- Distraction from focusing on developing disciples. Church leaders can become satisfied by the multitude which attends the larger gathering. The problem is that while it might appear that a lot is happening in the large crowd, often few disciples are formed. Why? Because discipleship does not primarily take place in the crowd or by people hearing God's word.

- Inactivity among attendees. Focusing on attendance produces inactivity among church attendees who feel like they've fulfilled their purpose by attending the large worship gathering. Those attending the worship gathering might or might not be disciples of Jesus Christ and because anonymity is promoted, no one really knows.

Christ never focused on the crowd while on earth. Yes, he did miracles and attracted a crowd, but he never concentrated on them as part of his long-term strategy. In fact, we see Jesus winnowing away the crowd by calling out disciples. Michael Wilkins dedicated his life to understand the meaning of discipleship. His main textbook on discipleship, *Following the Master*, is the most exhaustive on the subject. He writes,

"The objective of Jesus' ministry among the crowd was to make them disciples. As he taught and preached, the sign of faith was when one came out of the crowd and called Jesus 'Lord' (Mt 8:18-21)." [5] Jesus knew the crowd was fickle. He wanted long-term personal commitment, not temporary relief because of the miracles. John Eldredge, a famous author who also leads a house church, writes,

> Going to church with hundreds of other people to sit and hear a sermon doesn't ask much of you. It certainly will never expose you. That's why most folks prefer it. Because community will. It will reveal where you have yet to become holy. It will bring you close and you will be seen and you will be known, and therein lies the power and therein lies the danger. [6]

Some church strategists teach that leaders must first attract a crowd in order to make disciples, but Jesus didn't do this. He often discouraged the crowd from following him for impure motivations and exhorted them to count the cost of following him. Robert Coleman in *The Master Plan of Evangelism* writes,

> Most of the evangelistic efforts of the church begin with the multitude under the assumption that the church is qualified to conserve what good is done. The result is our spectacular emphasis upon numbers of converts, candidates for baptism, and more members for the church, with little or no genuine concern manifested toward the establishment of these souls in the love and power of God, let alone the preservation and continuation of the work. [7]

Although many in the cell church vision have realized that attendance should not be the focus, they are often trapped by other pitfalls that don't adequately motivate over the long haul.

THE INADEQUACY OF CELL GROUP
ATTENDANCE GROWTH

Cell group attendance growth is distinct from "Sunday attendance growth" because it emphasizes attendance in both a small group and a large group—not just the larger worship service. Growth in both cell and celebration is a step in the right direction, but it is still inadequate.

Many pastors embrace cell ministry because they want to be like the largest churches in the world. In fact, most of the model cell churches today were inspired by Yoido Full Gospel Church in Seoul, Korea, which is the pioneer of the modern cell church movement. YFGC grew to become the largest church in the history of Christianity.

Founder David Cho, and lead pastor of YFGC until very recently, implemented cell ministry as the base of the church back in the early 1970s, and the church grew to about twenty-five thousand cells, two hundred fifty thousand in attendance, and some eight hundred fifty-thousand members (and many, many church plants worldwide). [8] YFGC inspired the possibility of unlimited growth, and many pastors have made their pilgrimage to YFGC to discover how this church works. Some of those who implemented Cho's model have become mega-cell churches, like the Elim Church in El Salvador. Elim started their cell journey in 1986 after visiting YFGC and has not stopped growing. Many others have had similar results.

Then why is cell church growth a poor motivation for doing cell ministry? Here are some reasons:

1.   Turning ministry into techniques

When a church enters into the cell church vision because of the possibility of growth, it's easy to look to techniques, rather than God, to bring the growth. Many jump into cell ministry to achieve growth like YFGC, and the vast majority of churches are disappointed when the growth simply doesn't happen. The reality is that only Jesus can bring qualitative, lasting growth. Leaders can often superficially think that following a 1-2-3 step approach will bring desired results. Perhaps information obtained at a seminar at a growing model church led them to believe in guaranteed success. The reality is that only God can produce lasting, eternal growth.

2.   Losing focus on the quality of the disciples

Quality is harder to measure than quantity. If a leader spotlights the number of people attending the cells or larger gatherings, he or she will often miss the more qualitative reasons for cell ministry. For example, many overlook whether the cells are actually practicing community or attempting outreach. When a leader doesn't understand the biblical purpose behind cell ministry, it's easy to fall into the trap of emphasis on outward results, which normally produces disappointment and disillusionment.

3.   Disappointment when expectations aren't met

Most leaders are not satisfied by their church's growth rate. They want their churches to grow much faster than what is currently happening. When they jump into cell ministry with the expectation that their church will grow like Yoido Full Gospel Church or one of the other exciting cell churches, they can easily become condemned and discouraged. Often the church will then set aside cell ministry for another program or model.

While we should rejoice in what God has done through David Cho and growing churches like YFGC, the motivation that comes from exciting church growth is inadequate. The reality is that very few churches will grow to megachurch status, and those which do have a unique, rare combination of giftedness, talent, and positive external factors (e.g., receptivity in country, and so forth). What happens to the cell churches that experience slow growth? Should they move on to another model? If cell church growth is the reason and motivating factor, they should move on.

4. Faulty Leadership Style

One very subtle result of being motivated by cell church growth is embracing a wrong leadership style. Sometimes to "get results" leaders become controlling, domineering, and start demanding that members produce great numbers. Often the leaders behave this way because they *thought* this was the key to someone's successful model. Because the *model church* seemed to behave that way, they also implemented that leadership style.

I know one pastor who has the reputation of motivating his people through *terror*, rather than humble godly service. *Terror* was the word used by his denominational supervisor, and I had to agree with this supervisor after having spent time in this pastor's church. Did this pastor produce growth? Yes. But it wasn't growth based on a biblical motivation, and such growth was not qualitative and won't stand the test of time.

THE INADEQUACY OF EASY IMPLEMENTATION

Pastors and leaders are busy. While they understand that principles are important, in the milieu of a busy lifestyle, they often prefer a package right off the shelf that can be unwrapped and easily followed.

In one sense there's nothing wrong with this, especially when starting out. A church needs a pattern, at least to begin with.

But what I call "easy implementation" can have disastrous consequences in the long haul. Why?

1. Transferability Problems

Often a packaged model doesn't work in any other context than where it was created. It might seem easier initially to just "plug and play," but the model ends up malfunctioning because of cultural barriers. For example, how would a cell church model formed in the inner city of Manila work in the rural environment of South Dakota? Or how does a model forged in a group-oriented atmosphere in Africa work in the individualistic culture of Australia?

There's also the denominational context. One model might work great among the Assembly of God in Brazil but not work at all among the Baptists in Spain. What worked great in a Latin American Pentecostal environment where leaders are more authoritative will need to be adapted among Baptists who follow a more congregational, participatory form of governance.

When enough of these obstacles occur due to transferability problems, the packaged cell model is often shelved and forgotten, and the underlying thinking is that cell ministry doesn't work. The problem was not the cell strategy but the wholesale adoption of someone else's model.

2.   Lack of creativity

God is a creative God. He delights when his children seek him and draw from his bountiful creativity. Following someone else's model thwarts the pastor from depending on God's innovative guidance. Following someone else's model is superficial and doesn't stir the church leaders to look to God for the power to innovate. Rather, the leader is glued to the manual produced by someone else's ingenuity and is always asking, what would the creator of this model do?

When the leader wants to change direction or tweak the packaged model, he or she won't know what to do because the original creative idea came from someone else who understood how to adapt as circumstances changed.

3. Lack of motivation

One of the main problems with following someone else's model is the lack of incentive. Over time, the leaders wonder why they put so much effort into doing cell ministry—especially when the results are not immediately visible. The church leadership begins to doubt all the extra time it takes to fine-tune the cell groups, practice discipleship equipping, and coach existing leaders.

Over time, it becomes exceedingly hard to motivate and mobilize the congregation to press ahead with cell ministry. Why? Because the motivation based on someone else's growth doesn't excite the imagination. When leaders get tired and obstacles occur, the leader quits midstream, thinking that cell church simply didn't work, when in reality following a model didn't work.

4. Becoming a slave of someone else

Some model cell churches require total obedience in exchange for new information about their model. They say that the key to successful implementation of their model is to also come under their covering, which is often a code word for control.

A modern day example of this is the International Charismatic Mission in Bogota, Columbia. This church exploded with growth in the 1990s and became a worldwide sensation. ICM asked everyone to follow their entire model, rather than principles that could be adapted and adjusted for changing circumstances. They required churches to come under their apostolic covering to then receive inside information. Many churches left their denominations, causing painful divisions. One of their secrets was the importance of the number twelve as being critical to cell success, which also supposedly came with a special anointing. [9]

Today, most churches have seen the inadequacy of wholeheartedly following models like G12 and have gained new freedom and effectiveness by adapting the principles to their own church context.

THE INADEQUACY OF UNDERDEVELOPED THEOLOGY

Ralph Neighbour is famous for coining the phrase, "Theology breeds methodology." Yet, many pastors don't have a strong theological foundation for cell ministry. Perhaps they started cell ministry because they saw the lack of pastoral care in their church, and they tried to plug the pastoral hole with a few small groups. Cell ministry was simply another program rather than the heart of the church. Many churches establish their small groups on the oft quoted passage in Acts 2:42-46,

> They devoted themselves to the apostles' teaching and to fellowship, to the breaking of bread and to prayer. Everyone was filled with awe, and many wonders and miraculous signs were done by the apostles. All the believers were together and had everything in common. Selling their possessions and goods, they gave to anyone as he had need. Every day they continued to meet together in the temple courts. They broke bread in their homes and ate together with glad and sincere hearts.

This wonderful text has helped the church understand the connection between cells and celebration in the Jerusalem church. [10] Yet, these verses give little information about cell and celebration, and they don't provide a strong enough foundation to carry a church through the storms of ministry. In other words, it's not deep enough. So what is the problem with not having a deeper biblical reason for doing cell ministry? Sustainability.

If the foundation is superficial, there's a good chance that cell ministry will not withstand the storms of doubt, resistance, and weariness. Cell leaders, supervisors, and staff might give up when the going gets tough or an apparently easier program comes along. If the motivation isn't firmly linked to biblical truth, it's natural to view cell ministry as just another program.

For many years I was more excited about the pragmatic reasons for cell ministry and promoted key methodologies to help churches grow through cell ministry. Yet I didn't prioritize the biblical base for cell ministry enough. As the years have passed, I've realized the necessity of starting with a strong theological base. I made it a priority to answer for myself the theological questions for cell ministry and in 2012 I wrote a book called, *Biblical Foundations for the Cell-Based Church*. In this book I lay out key biblical foundations for doing cell ministry, which include:

- The triune nature of God. God created humankind in his image, which is inherently relational. Isolationism goes against God's nature, and God calls his church to reflect community. God is working within believers to make them more relational.
- The Church as the family of God. God created families to reflect his triune nature. The image of family is the primary metaphor for life in the New Testament church. God forged the Church, his new family, in houses to

reflect a close-knit, *one another* relationship, where hospitality and the extended family was the priority.

- Christ's emphasis on the home. Jesus Christ came to proclaim God's rule, his kingdom. Christ gathered a community of disciples to demonstrate how this new kingdom operated. He chose ministry in homes to reflect the image of the new family of God. He then sent his disciples in teams to minister in houses, giving them clear instructions on how to reach people through the house strategy.

- The house church environment of the early Church. God established the early church in the house environment, which spread over the entire Roman Empire. Most house churches were between ten to twenty people, although some house churches were larger. The content of the house meetings was flexible and dynamic. They celebrated the Lord's supper as a meal, enjoyed fellowship, ministered to one another from the word of God, practiced hospitality, prayed, worshipped, baptized new believers, and evangelized.

- Relational evangelism through close contacts that extended from the house churches. The gospel flowed via the extended family in New Testament times, which included immediate relatives, servants, freemen, hired workers, and sometimes tenants and partners in a trade. As Jesus transformed people, they behaved differently within their family relationships. Husbands cared for their wives, slaves were treated with dignity, married partners submitted to one another, and love ruled. People could see the changes up close as city life was lived out in the open, and many became followers of Jesus and his new family.

- Organic leadership development from house to house ministry. Christ's apostles led the Church after Pentecost, but the early Church began relying on leaders developed through house church ministry. Leadership in the early Church was organic, charismatic, non-hierarchical, home based, team-oriented, and promoted both males and females. The Spirit of God through his gifts allowed each member to minister. Females played an essential role in early leadership, and the focus was on the team, rather than one leader.

- The connection between house churches. The early church primarily met in house churches, but those house churches were not independent entities. At times the house churches gathered regularly together for larger meetings, as we can see in both Jerusalem and Corinth. At other times those gatherings were less frequent. The New Testament writers used the word *ecclesia* to refer to the house church gatherings, the large gatherings, and the universal Church.

While these principles come directly from scripture, I also know that it's possible to get lost in the maze of biblical reasons for cell church ministry. Is it possible to narrow these principles down into one main purpose? Is there one motivation that stands above the rest? I believe there is and explaining that purpose is the main reason for writing this book.

THE INADEQUACY OF MORE LEADERS

For many years, I thought leadership development was the essence of cell ministry. I took the passage in Matthew 9:37-38 as my starting point where Jesus said to his disciples, "The harvest is plentiful but the workers are few. Ask the Lord of the harvest, therefore, to send out workers into his harvest field."

Yet, I began to see holes in my use of the word *leader* in 2001. I held the view that everyone in the church should become a leader, but a few pastors challenged me on this. Pastor Dave, a gifted teacher and a very analytical person, realized that many lay people in his own church didn't want to become leaders. He especially wanted to know whether the leadership conviction, expressed in my book *Leadership Explosion* was biblical.[1] Dave, along with the other pastors in the coaching group, wrestled with this issue, wanting to know how biblical the word *leader* was. They didn't feel there was sufficient biblical evidence for prioritizing *leadership* through cell ministry. I also came to realize that the Bible didn't directly say that everyone should become a *leader*. It was a great concept, but it was simply hard to defend.

Then there was the problem with the definition of a *leader*. Many cultures viewed leaders as controlling and dominating. For many, the word *leader* conjured images of a special type of person who is gifted to direct others, create followers, and boldly envision the future. Others imagine that a Christian *leader* must hold an official position in the church. In other words, a leader seemed to be beyond the reach of most lay people.

Dave discouraged me from using the word *leader* in the discipleship equipping process. He felt the word *disciple* squared with scripture far better than leader. I had been using the word *leader* for so long that I resisted his argument but something rang true in Dave's argument as I examined scripture.

I realized that Dave's point coincided with Jesus and his disciples. Jesus himself used the word *disciple* to describe his followers. Jesus transformed the world by telling his disciples that the greatest would be one who served the most (Luke 22:26). He took off his garments and washed the feet of his

---

1 In **Leadership Explosion**, I made the case for developing leaders through cell groups. In that book I interact with leadership theory and what the Bible says about leadership.

disciples to model servanthood. God began to change me and help me to grasp a more biblical basis for the essence of cell ministry.

A MOTIVATION THAT STANDS THE TEST OF TIME

Christ's clear command to the church was to make disciples who make disciples. He gave the Church "marching orders" in Matthew 28:18-20 when he said,

> All authority in heaven and on earth has been given to me. Therefore go and make disciples of all nations, baptizing them in the name of the Father and of the Son and of the Holy Spirit, and teaching them to obey everything I have commanded you. And surely I am with you always, to the very end of the age.

In Matthew 28, Jesus is telling his own group of disciples to develop another group of disciples. Jesus expected his disciples to follow his pattern of exemplifying his power and love through practical teaching and examples. Jesus developed his own group of twelve and hung out with them for three years. In the atmosphere of the group, these disciples were molded, shaped, trained, and then sent forth. The same disciples became the key leaders of the early Church. Christ's purpose in molding them in the small group had a greater purpose.

Not only did Jesus minister with these disciples over the course of three years, but he then sent them into the homes to establish house churches that would multiply and infiltrate the surrounding communities (Luke 9 and 10).

The word *disciple* occurs two hundred thirty-two times in the Gospels and twenty-seven times in the book of Acts—a total of two hundred fifty-nine times. The word *disciple* simply means pupil or learner.[11] In ancient times, a teacher's students or followers were called disciples and behaved in much the same manner as those who followed Jesus (Matthew 5:1; Luke 6:17; 19:37). There were many learners of Jesus in the New Testament but only some became his disciples—those who chose to obey Christ's teaching.

After Christ's resurrection, the word *disciple* was replaced by words such as *believer, saint, Christian, brother* or *sister* in Christ. Why? Because after Pentecost, God established the Church, the gathering of believers, to be the main place where discipleship occurred. Rather than becoming a disciple of one person, the early Christians were molded and shaped by the Spirit of God working through Christ's Church. The early Church followed Christ's pattern and changed the world house by house. Those house churches celebrated together. Michael Wilkens says, "Discipling today is always undertaken as an outgrowth of the life of the church, whereas prior to Pentecost it occurred with Jesus personally. . . We may go so far as to say that in many ways discipleship is the overall goal of the church, including evangelism, nurturing, fellowship, leadership, worship, etc."[12] God chose the Church to make disciples—both today and in New Testament times.

Cell ministry isn't primarily about the cell but making disciples who are molded, shaped, and transformed through the cell system. As leaders understand this process, a new, purer motivation develops that compels the pastor forward because of a new understanding of the *why* of cell ministry. Understanding that the cell strategy is primarily about making disciples places cell ministry within the biblical framework and encourages pastors to stop focusing on outward models and to prioritize a secure biblical anchor for ministry.

Chapter Two

SO WHY CELLS?

In preparation for writing this book, I scoured all the books I could find on *discipleship*. I expected the authors to highlight Christ's call to make disciples in a small group as well as the early church's commitment to follow that pattern through house-to-house ministry. However, I was amazed at how many books skipped over Christ's call to discipleship in a group. Most, in fact, emphasized personal growth and the one-on-one variety of discipleship found in individualistic western cultures, like North America.

The typical pattern found in most of these discipleship books is to start with Jesus and the need for discipleship. The writers will then define the word *disciple*, explain the importance of discipleship, and elucidate the differences between discipleship in Christ's time from the post-resurrection Church.

Then the book will jump to current methods of discipleship, such as personal spirituality and one-on-one discipleship. The author will discuss the need to practice the spiritual disciplines, like having a quiet time, fasting, prayer, Bible reading, and other disciplines of the Christian life. Later on in the book, the author might have a chapter about the necessity of belonging to a local church as an important factor of discipleship.

Yet, the primary way discipleship plays out practically in these books is through personal growth between God and the potential disciple and entering a one-on-one discipleship relationship with a mature Christian. Often ministries emphasizing one-on-one discipleship, such as Navigators, Campus Crusade, or InterVarsity, are highlighted as examples of how to do this.

I have always believed strongly in spiritual disciplines and have been discipled one-on-one various times. I'm not in disagreement with what these authors write. My only concern is whether this is what Jesus had in mind.

What amazes me is the lack of material about discipleship in a group. Books on discipleship don't connect how Jesus and the early Church made disciples with how we should be discipling today. Most authors fail to explain the group context of discipleship in the New Testament and make it seem like the individual variety is the biblical way to make disciples. To ignore this and jump into personal devotions or one-on-one discipleship leaps from biblical times to the western culture.

Why do so many authors do this? Because most books on discipleship are written by authors who are from individualistic cultures, where the assumption is that the individual takes precedence over the group. However, this is not true from Church history or even for the majority of cultures today.

DISCIPLESHIP ACCORDING TO JESUS

Scripture says, "Then the eleven disciples went to Galilee, to the mountain where Jesus had told them to go. When they saw him, they worshiped him; but some doubted. Then Jesus came to them and said, 'All authority in heaven and on earth has been given to me. Therefore go and make disciples of all nations, baptizing them in the name of the Father and of the Son and of the Holy Spirit, and teaching them to obey everything I have commanded you. And surely I am with you always, to the very end of the age'" (Matthew 28:16-20).

Notice that Jesus is talking to the group of disciples in these verses. These are the same disciples (apart from Judas) who Jesus molded and shaped for a three-year period. He had taught them important life lessons as they lived together. Much of the crucial character development came as they worked through conflicts and overcame difficulties with one another. Jesus had called these disciples to join a new community and become part of a new spiritual family. [13] They learned how to relate to one another through the crucible of conflict. Jesus checked their pride, encouraging them to walk in humility. After three years, they were ready to start the process once again with their own small group. They understood that following Jesus meant public confession and a group commitment.

The disciples certainly had a personal relationship with God, but that personal relationship needed to be molded and shaped in a community atmosphere where the one-anothers of scripture were prioritized (more on the one-anothers in the next chapter). Jesus said to his disciples, "A new command I give you: Love one another. As I have loved you, so you must love one another. By this all men will know that you are my disciples, if you love one another" (John 13:34-35).

Jesus used the home to gather his Church, the new family of God. I sometimes picture Jesus sleeping around campfires, like images of cowboys in the wild, wild West. Yet Jesus ministered in a household setting. When reading about Jesus going from village to village and healing the sick, he was actually ministering in homes. The following offers a glimpse of Christ's home ministry:

- Jesus in the house of Peter (Matthew 8:14)
- Jesus in the house of Matthew (Matthew 9:10)
- Jesus in the house of Zacchaeus (Luke 19:1-10)
- Jesus in the house of Lazarus and his sisters (Luke 10:38-42)
- Jesus in the house of Jairus (Mark 5:35-38)
- Jesus healing two blind people in a house (Matthew 9:28-30)
- Jesus in the house of Simon the leper (Matthew 26:6)
- Jesus teaching his disciples in a house (Mark 7:17-18; 9:33; 10:10)
- Jesus forgiving and healing a paralyzed person in a house (Luke 5:19)
- Jesus in the home of a Pharisee (Luke 14:1)
- Jesus instituting the Lord's supper in a house (Matthew 26:18)
- Jesus sent his twelve and his seventy disciples to heal and teach from village to village and house-to-house (Luke 9:1-9; 10:1-11)

Jesus infiltrated the houses and families of his day to promote this new family of faith. He then sent his disciples two-by-two to minister in homes (Luke 9 and 10). After Christ's resurrection, the early Church met in houses to continue this family mentality.

Through house-to-house ministry, they turned the world upside down, from the inside out.

What does the Great Commission tell us? It says that God desires to transform people from lone individualists into team players. David Watson, Anglican evangelist and author, writes,

> It is equally striking that Jesus calls individuals, not to stay in isolation, but to join the new community of God's people. He called the Twelve to share their lives, with him and with each other. They were to live every day in a rich and diverse fellowship, losing independence, learning interdependence, gaining from each other new riches and strength. [14]

Relating to other people and learning to give and take is important to God. Yes, he does desire that each person have an individual relationship with him, but this is only part of the equation. Yet, according to most books on discipleship, one-on-one discipleship and a personal relationship with God are the essence of discipleship. Scripture tells us another story about discipleship.

THE BIBLICAL CONTEXT

When we talk about the Bible's inspiration, we are referring to the moment the writer's wrote down their words. At that moment, they were writing the very words of God. Everything afterwards is application of what they wrote. For this reason, it's essential to know to whom they were writing, the context and culture in which they were writing, and the general history of the time period. Afterwards, it's possible to correctly interpret the passage and apply it accurately.

Yet, many people skip this point. They jump right into the application of scripture without obtaining the correct interpretation to begin with. To understand the New Testament writers, we need to understand the context.

The context of the New Testament was a group atmosphere. Those in the New Testament times were part of a collective culture that prioritized the group more than the individual. Dr. Joseph Hellerman, professor at Talbot Theological Seminary, writes, "This strong-group perspective runs throughout both the Old and New Testaments. It has been God's design from the beginning."[15] Jesus and the New Testament writers expected people to be part of a group. The culture that the authors of scripture wrote to resembled group oriented cultures today, like the African culture. Norman Kraus, Mennonite missionary and author, writing about the biblical context, says,

> The cultural background against which it should be interpreted more closely resembles some contemporary African tribal cultures than American individualism. In these societies the individual is viewed as a particular embodiment of the organic family, literally tied to the ancestors as the continuation of their life force. The individual gains self-identity by assimilating the identity of the clan.[16]

The New Testament writers would not have understood modern individualism. For them, the individual was always a part of a larger social world and this social world was primary. In contrast, the Bible is predicated on the belief that human beings at every level are bound together in communities of various sorts. Church researcher, John Ellas writes,

Early Christian community stands in strong contrast to present conditions where church members have very limited interpersonal relationships. 'One another' ministry requires face-to-face spiritual interaction that is missing for the majority of members in churches today. In biblical community, members love, serve, pray, and carry one another's burdens (Gal 6:2). [17]

Rodney Clapp, author of a book on discipleship and popular culture, writes, "In historical perspective, it is our individuated, isolated self that is exceedingly strange." [18]

God chose the small group context to develop fully devoted followers of Jesus Christ, and he does the same thing today. This is the context God chose to build his church. Why? Because this is the context in which we can become fully devoted followers of Jesus Christ

GROUP DISCIPLESHIP AND CULTURE

Every culture contains good and bad elements, and all aspects of cultures need to be judged on whether they align with scripture. We must submit to the Bible and allow it to critique culture. No culture is perfect, but God's word is. Culture must conform to God's word and not the other way around. God desires to change us to conform to his word, and we must remember that the Bible, not culture, needs to dictate all that we do and think.

Cultures common to North America, Australia, and Europe are more individualistic in nature. There are many great traits of these western cultures, such as respect for rule of the law, hard work, creativity, diligence, and individual achievement. While there are many exemplary qualities, much of present day individualism has led down the dangerous path of isolationism, anonymity, and loneliness.

The culture of individualism is uncomfortable with biblical commands to serve one another, submit to others, give up rights for the greater good of the group, and to humble oneself before others. Yet, these biblical traits are absolutely essential and foundational in scripture.[19] Christ's command to his disciples is clear: love one another. The triune God is a timeless testimony of God's unity. The early Church was a *face-to-face* movement, meeting in homes and multiplying God's life through community.

The group-oriented context of the New Testament and the many exhortations to follow the one-anothers and walk in unity indicate that God wants to shape disciples in a group context. Whether a culture does this well is not the main point. What is essential is the willingness to be molded and conformed to what God says is important.

Western individualistic cultures cannot justify scripturally that Jesus is focusing on one-on-one discipleship when he clearly demonstrated what type of discipleship he's promoting.

We must be true to scripture and first promote the way of discipleship found in the pages of scripture and then apply other aspects of discipleship to our own culture, without trying to read into scripture what is not there. Scripture, not culture determines the motivation for doing cell ministry.

As mentioned earlier, the main reason the church has missed this theme of community in the western world is because too often believers read the Bible through the lens of individualism. The reality is that those living in a collectivist culture understand group discipleship much better because they already innately prioritize relationships. They are also much more comfortable in a group setting and take less time to warm up.

I've been a missionary for many years in a group-oriented culture and do most of my current cell seminars in group oriented cultures. I've discovered that these cultures are naturally more comfortable in a group setting because they are naturally community oriented. One very positive aspect of group-oriented cultures is the propensity toward community. Our small group ministry in Ecuador, for example, grew rapidly among a far more group-oriented culture. People in the church were excited to participate in the groups because they generally liked being with other people and counted it as a priority. It wasn't hard to gather people together in the relaxed atmosphere of the home because this was their inward desire.

The reality is that the God of community has blessed most cultures around the world with a group orientation. Theologian Bruce J. Malina writes, "Some 80 percent of the people on our planet are collectivist... The significant fact for those individualists who read the Bible is that biblical writers and the people they depict were also collectivists, including Jesus." [20] Malina goes on to say, "Individualist cultures are a rather recent phenomenon."[21] They didn't exist before the sixteenth or seventeenth century, according to Malina.

Individualism is not the norm, especially those aspects that tend to withdraw from others and separate from community. I do realize that establishing small group ministry is more difficult in individualistic culture because of the tendency to pull away rather than prioritize relationships. Yet, whether individualistic or group oriented, scripture still stands true and exhorts us to make disciples in a group.

In researching and practicing cell ministry in the United States and other western countries, I have noticed that people don't naturally connect in small groups. It takes a longer time for community to develop. Multiplication also takes longer because the group needs time to become a community, the family of God. Western cultures have to work at community and most find it harder to be a regular part of a cell group. I've heard many western leaders, in fact, say, "Small groups are just not my thing," or "They might be for others—the touchy-feely type person—but not for me. I'm just built differently. I feel uncomfortable in a group." I chuckle when I hear this because I now believe that most westerners feel uncomfortable in a group. But can we use this cultural line of reasoning to avoid small group involvement? Biblical discipleship, rather, requires that we journey within a small group and allow God to mold us in the process.

The reality is that cell groups might not work well. Relationships are messy. People are dysfunctional. We are selfish and want to follow our own path. Some in the group tend to talk too much and don't listen sufficiently. Others hide and don't express themselves. Yet, all cultures, regardless of being group-oriented or individualistic, need community discipleship. God has chosen this method to make us more like Jesus.

INDIVIDUAL EXPRESSION IN A GROUP

Concentrating on community shouldn't take away from the individual's worth but rather should enhance it. Individuals who are being molded within a small community of believers continue to grow in a personal relationship with God.

The Trinity is our example here. Perfect unity exists within the Trinity, but each person of the Godhead is unique. The Bible underlines two complementary and equally important truths in this area. On the one hand, it emphasizes the intrinsic worth of the individual, as made in the image of God. On the other hand, the Bible places great emphasis on the importance of community.[22]

We also need to distinguish between individuality and individualism. Individuality refers to an individual as a responsible person in community, while individualism exalts the independence of individuals and their private rights. Individuality can be good, while individualism breeds alienation and pride. Kraus says, "The sin of humankind is not the assertion of individuality in community, but the assertion of individual self-sufficiency and independence from God and fellow humans."[23]

The biblical alternative is the individual in community. It's having a relationship with God but then being in community with the body of Christ. Each group member depends on the other and is involved with each other. This interaction enhances individual personhood and provides personal identity.[24]

God allows us to be all we are supposed to be in community. We become strong as individuals as we relate to others in the group. All of Christ's disciples had strong personalities, but they learned through conflict to submit to one another. That's the goal of being molded through the community process.

Knowing and experiencing God is profoundly conditioned by the community. Our continuing relation to him is sustained and nurtured in community. Our convictions are expressed, caring takes place, as well as forgiving and receiving forgiveness. David Gill, author and professor of Christian ethics, writes:

> We must have the community to support and correct our discipleship in the world. This seems so obvious, but our practice is so frequently individualistic. Christian discipleship is not for Lone Rangers (though in all fairness, even the masked man had Tonto as his sidekick). We must resist the individualism of our culture and cultivate deep and strong relationships with others. The challenges we face are formidable; without community they become impossible.[25]

In a healthy small group not only is our individuality maintained, but we realize that we are valued individuals with a God-assigned role to play. Discipleship in a group includes interdependent and reciprocal relationships, which aim at enhancing the personal quality of the group itself. What people have in common is each other and the mutual enhancement of each person as they live out their lives together.[26] Group discipleship is not an emptying of my own rights, aspirations, or goals. Rather, it's developing those personal attributes in the group atmosphere.

We become disciples as we learn to love one another and allow others to hold us accountable. This was the type of discipleship Jesus had in mind when he commanded his disciples to continue his own strategy for disciple-making in the group environment.

Part 2

HOW CELLS MAKE DISCIPLES

Chapter Three

DISCIPLESHIP THROUGH COMMUNITY

Jim had little interest in *following* Jesus, but after many friendly conversations, he was finally ready to *hear* about Jesus. One night while talking at his house, he even prayed the "sinner's prayer." However, I did not see any change in his life, and I wondered if he was truly born-again. He maintained his individual version of Christianity, telling me that he was a very private person and didn't like to open up to other people. After many months of just listening and praying for Jim, I felt the need to challenge his false, individualistic thinking. I said to him, "Those who know Jesus are willing for others to hold them accountable. They don't hold on to a privatized religion and their own personal faith." My words hit a wall. Jim didn't mind hearing about Jesus and was willing to even "accept Christ." But to become a responsible member of the body of Christ was far, far from his mind or desire. Jim, like so many others, had bought into a privatized view of Christianity—me and God.

On the contrary, God's work is not complete in a person until the private, personal space has been invaded, and he or she is willing to be forged on the anvil of community. The apostle John said, "But if we walk in the light, as he is in the light, we have fellowship with one another, and the blood of Jesus, his Son, purifies us from all sin" (1 John 1:7). Community or *koinonia* (the Greek word for *fellowship*) refers to our relationship with God and to our relationship with one another.

Koinonia is the fellowship that we have with the Trinity that needs to be practiced with other believers. An exclusive personal relationship with God is foreign to New Testament Christianity. While it might be foreign to the New Testament, it's quite common in many churches. Author and pastor, Tod Bolsinger, heard this individualistic message while growing up. He writes,

> What most of us heard in those kinds of messages is that we can have a personal and private relationship with Christ. I remember the youth leader giving an invitation and saying, "There is nothing to join, you don't have to be a church member. It's just about having a relationship with Jesus." And I wanted that. Not church, but Jesus. Shortly after I committed my life to following Christ, I bought a T-shirt that said "JC and me." It was a not-so-subtle way of sharing my faith, and it described my new-found belief perfectly. This wasn't my parents' religion, this wasn't about tradition or ritual, it was about "JC and me"—a sentiment that always sounds good until you start reading the Bible.[27]

Notice the last part of Bolsinger's words, "a sentiment that always sounds good until you start reading the Bible." What might sound cool in an individualistic culture is very foreign to a biblical view of community. Too often we've acted like we don't need the church.

There's even a movement today that says, "Love Jesus; hate the church." I think I understand the movement's motivation to win back people who have been turned off by a carnal church. Yet, their motto repulses me every time I hear it because we need to love the Church, in spite of her shortcomings. God chose the Church to make disciples. Christ's precious bride is God's instrument to help believers grow in their sanctification. We are saved by Jesus but then molded through community in his Church to become Christ's disciples.

The larger gathering that most of us have come to experience on Sunday morning doesn't facilitate community as does a small group of three to fifteen people. While both are needed, the power of the small group is to bolster and strengthen community and help each person develop relationships. The cell provides a smaller accountability structure that allows deeper relationships to develop.

BECOMING LIKE GOD

Each person in the Trinity lives in perfect harmony with the other two. God is not a lone ranger but relates in a group. And since God's plan is to make us like himself (Romans 8:29), his goal is to mold and transform us through others. Rodney Clapp writes, "We are made in the image of a Trinitarian, communal God. We depend on others to be born, to survive, to be buried and remembered. We live and have our being in community, however, attenuated it may become."[28] It might be alien to individualistic cultures but God, the Trinity, desires to mold and shape us to conform to his Trinitarian nature.

When Jesus was on earth he was constantly telling his disciples about the unity he had with the Father and the Spirit. He also asked them to demonstrate that same love and unity so that the world might believe. He said to his Father, "My prayer is not for them alone. I pray also for those who will believe in me through their message, that all of them may be one, Father, just as you are in me and I am in you. May they also be in us so that the world may believe that you have sent me" (John 17:21-22).

God's plan for the Church is clear in Christ's prayer. He desires the Church to live in unity and walk in love, so that others might trust in him and believe the message. Richard Meyers, researcher on Christian community, writes, "God not only enjoys community, models community, and builds community, but also God commands community."[29] God models the community he wants us to follow. As we understand who he is and the love that comes from the Trinity, we will allow him to make us relational disciples.

Small groups help in the discipleship process of becoming like the Trinity by helping members to take off their masks and enter into each other's lives, while allowing love to rule. If a church is only meeting in the larger gathering, it's easier for people to remain superficial and leave in anonymity.

It is difficult to remain isolated in a cell group setting. Last night at my own men's life group, we didn't have a perfect experience. In fact, it was messy. Certain ones talked too much. Others talked too little. But the beauty of the group was the interaction we experienced as members of the body of Christ. We shared life together. I had a burden on my heart and needed counsel, so I brought it up to the rest of the group. I went away with new wisdom about the situation. They continue to hold me accountable. I grew as a disciple and will continue to mature as I walk with these brothers. I'm amazed how much I grow in the cell environment through honest and open sharing.

Have you noticed how many times the Bible tells us to be involved in each other's lives? In fact, the phrase one another appears one hundred times in the New Testament and fifty-eight of those occurrences have to do with relationships between believers and how to cultivate those relationships. Some of the more popular ones are:

- "A new command I give you: Love one another. As I have loved you, so you must love one another. By this all men will know that you are my disciples, if you love one another" (John 13:34-35).
- "Forgive as the Lord forgave you" (Colossians 3:13).
- "Therefore encourage one another and build each other up, just as in fact you are doing" (1 Thessalonians 5:11).
- "Be kind and compassionate to one another" (Ephesians 4:32).
- "Be devoted to one another in brotherly love" (Romans 12:10) [The word devoted might be translated "kindly affectionate." Paul had the devotion of a family in mind].
- "Submit to one another out of reverence for Christ" (Ephesians 5:21).
- "Therefore confess your sins to each other and pray for each other so that you may be healed. The prayer of a righteous man is powerful and effective" (James 5:16).

There are many, many more. Small groups are the atmosphere in which the early believers were shaped and molded to practice these one-anothers, and it's still the best way to practice them today. Stephen Macchia, founding president of Leadership Transformation, writes, "The healthy disciple understands that the 'one anothers' are not optional for the Christian life. They are community-building mandates from God to his people. His longing is for us to live in such vibrant Christian community that we can't help but shine brightly in juxtaposition to how others live in this world." [30]

Starting small groups does not guarantee community; it does, however, provide a conducive environment for spiritual relationships to be developed and for disciples to practice the one-anothers of scripture and to grow to be like the Trinity in the process. Larry Crabb, prolific author and psychologist, writes,

> We were designed by our Trinitarian God (who is Himself a group of three persons in profound relationship with each other) to live in relationship. Without it, we die. It's that simple. Without a community where we know, explore, discover, and touch one another, we experience isolation and despair that drive us in wrong directions that corrupt our efforts to live meaningfully and to love well. [31]

Most of us in the western world have difficulty with community. The good news is that the Trinity is the one who is molding us to become more like him as we relate to others. He is working through each member of his church to help us fulfill the one-anothers of scripture. I can just hear him cheering in the background, "Great job, Jim, you're working through that conflict with Jake. Don't run." Or "Don't stop attending the group, Tina, Linda needs to hear your story."

It's clear from scripture that Jesus asks us to be part of a group and that this is his vehicle for us to grow and develop as his disciples. We need the interaction with others to grow as believers. We need the interpersonal conflict that refines us and makes us more like Jesus. How will we respond to the interpersonal conflict? Will we become angry? Leave the group? Or work through the problem and become more like Jesus?

MOLDED IN THE FIRE

The disciples were formed and shaped in community as they learned together, laughed together, and experienced conflict together. Jesus knew that his followers had to go deep enough to take off their masks and be known. One of them even showed his true colors of deceit and deception and eventually betrayed him. David Watson writes, "In open and frequent fellowship with other Christians we can be sure that we are being real in following Jesus, and not just playing religious games, however correct our theology may be. Christianity is all about relationships: with God and with others." [32]

Christ gathered twelve disciples and journeyed with them for three years to demonstrate and teach them about love and community. Their lives were molded and shaped together, and this fiery fashioning of character became the main component of their training. In reality, Jesus had a huge challenge to unite such a diverse group. He brought together disciples who were temperamental and easily offended. They often saw each other as competitors. It wasn't easy for them to wash each other's feet (John 13:14).

Someone once said, "It's easy to find out if you love someone. Just get in a conflict and see what happens." To truly love, you'll have to overcome your hard feelings and ask God to help you practice the characteristics of love mentioned in 1 Corinthians 13:4-7:

Love is patient, love is kind. It does not envy, it does not boast, it is not proud. It is not rude, it is not self-seeking, it is not easily angered, it keeps no record of wrongs. Love does not delight in evil but rejoices with the truth. It always protects, always trusts, always hopes, always perseveres.

Those characteristics are best seen when the going gets tough. During my seminars I often get questions like, "What if I have someone in my group whom I don't get along with? What should I do?" Or "What if there are problem people in the group?" My normal response is something like, "Of course, you're going to have problem people in your group. Conflict in the group is normal. In fact, the conflict will make us more like Jesus. As we ask him for love and practice his forgiveness, we truly become his disciples."

On another occasion I answered a question about the best way to organize cell groups to avoid conflict. I understood the question and realized the intent was whether it was okay to find the "favorite" or "preferred" group. While I don't believe we should be forced to attend a particular group, I encouraged the asker to remember that "It's not all about my favorite group," or "hanging out with people I like." I reminded him that we become more like Jesus as we ask God for the strength to love one another and walk through the fire with others.

Many cell churches organize their groups geographically, while others arrange them based on homogeneity. There's no one way to do it. However, we do know that when members hop from group to group to avoid conflict, they're not allowing the Trinity to conform them into his image.

We need to allow normal conflict to mold and shape us. We must embrace it. God is molding us to be like him and part of that crucible is loving people who are different from us. The goal is to become like Jesus, and we do that as we work through conflict, rather than running from it. Discipleship demands that we pass through the fire while asking the Trinity to mold us and shape us to be like him.

Conflict reveals the group's hidden values, and assumptions that need to be examined. When people in the group know they can express both positive and negative feelings, their group experience will be genuine. New levels of understanding will flow as the group irons out differences. Someone said, "The group that fights together stays together."

What's the best way to deal with people in conflict? First, recognize the problem. Hiding it under a bush will only increase doubt among the members. Everyone knows it's there, so why hide it. You might say to an angry member, "I sense you're upset. We need to deal with this difference of opinion." Conflict can't be dealt with until it's recognized and brought into the open.

Second, pray. You won't solve the conflict without concerted prayer. You need to pray for wisdom and discernment.

Third, talk privately to the person with whom you are in conflict. I suggest you ask permission to start your conversation about a particular conflict. You might say, "Can I share something with you?" Then proceed to share with the person what's on your heart. Or, "When you used sarcasm to put me down in front of the group, I felt hurt and offended." As you work out your problems with those in your group, you'll grow to become more like Jesus, because Jesus himself told us to talk directly to our brother when a conflict develops.

If the issue is between you and someone else in the group, it's best to confront the person individually, using the Lord's own pattern: "If your brother sins against you, go and show him his fault, just between the two of you. If he listens to you, you have won your brother over" (Matthew 18:15). If the problem is with the group itself, talk to the group. Remember that unresolved conflicts are liabilities. Few things undermine a group faster than when several members grow frustrated with one another.

Dietrich Bonhoeffer is a great example of someone who didn't run from conflict. Rather, he ran into it. He chose to return to Germany in the midst of World War II, knowing full well the danger he faced. He could have stayed in America but chose, rather, to suffer with his fellow Germans. Bonhoeffer realized that the true, spiritual answer to the suffocating Nazi dictatorship was Christian community, where individuality and voluntary servanthood reigned. Even in the midst of godless obedience to Hitler, a believing Christian remnant came together to experience Trinitarian community. Bonhoeffer writes of this experience in *Life Together: A Discussion of Christian Fellowship,*

> ... the Christian needs another Christian. ... He needs him again and again when he becomes discouraged, for by himself he cannot help himself without belying the truth. He needs his brother man as a bearer and proclaimer of the divine word of salvation. He needs his brother solely because of Jesus Christ. The Christ in his own heart is weaker than the Christ in the word of his brother; his own heart is uncertain, his brother's is sure.[33]

We need each other to become more like Jesus as we grow through the fire of conflict, rather than fleeing from it. Most people flee conflict, thinking it will be easier somewhere else. The truth, however, is that the grass is rarely greener on the other side. Problems have the way of cropping up in other forms and in other situations.

NO PLACE LIKE HOME

When a person feels the warmth of family love and security, healing flows more freely. I think of Tim, a new believer who entered our church doors directly from prison. His wife had already been attending with their children, and we waited with anticipation for the day that Tim would show up. That day came after about one year later. Tim was abused as a child and never felt loved or wanted by his parents. He was tossed around from home to home and from father to father.

Tim plugged into a cell group and his transformation took a long, long time. I remember the days right after his release from prison when his words and demeanor were very rough indeed. Yet, we've seen Tim transformed before our eyes. Although he had been in churches previously, he never had experienced the love of a family—brothers and sisters who were willing to talk directly and openly with him. Tim has testified on various occasions in the larger gathering that he never knew a true family until his experience in a cell group. Community has the power to change lives.

"The family of God" and "household of God" are both used in the New Testament to describe Christ's church. These two terms are the principal church images of the New Testament. In writing to Timothy, Paul referred to the Church as the "household of God" (1 Timothy 3:15). He used the same language in writing to the Ephesian Christians (Ephesians 2:19). In Galatians 6:10, Paul changed the language slightly and referred to the church as the "household of faith." Families care for one another. They work together. They watch out for each other. You might say, "They watch each other's back." They walk the long journey together because they are part of a community that will last forever. Gilbert Bilezikian says it well,

> The biblical metaphor of "family" more appropriately describes what the church should resemble—a group of people, few enough in numbers to sit around in a circle, facing each other and sharing the joy and the benefits of togetherness. Every church that aspires to function as community must make a small group structure available to its constituency.[34]

God chose the house churches to bolster the family image in scripture. The gospel first began to transform those in the home and then continued to flow through the extended family lines.

The concept of family meshes consistently with Christ's command to make disciples. The family atmosphere is never an end in itself. Rather, a healthy family nurtures, protects, counsels, loves, tells the truth, and then sends out the sons and daughters to form new families. Parents who don't prepare their children for the future don't have their children's best interest in mind. They are not making "healthy family members."

Gerhard Lohfink, renowned New Testament scholar, writes, "Jesus did indeed demand of his disciples that they leave everything, but he did not call them into solitude and isolation. That is not the point of discipleship. He called them into a new family of brothers and sisters, itself a sign of the arriving kingdom." [35] I like the way Lohfink combines discipleship with God's family. In reality, the image of the Church as God's family and Christ's call to disciple-making have the same intention in mind.

My wife and I desire that all three of our girls become responsible adults and eventually establish their own families. Of course, we will always love them and welcome them into our home. As family, they have the same rights as we do. When they were little children, we took care of them completely. Yet, we never wanted to make them dependent on us. We've always wanted them to go forth and become responsible, interdependent adults who are guiding their own lives and destinies.

David Jaramillo, pastor and psychologist, connects discipleship with family in a winsome way,

When I think of discipleship, the parent-child relationship comes to mind. In fact, the word "discipline" comes from the word "disciple," which means "learner." That is, it takes discipline to make disciples of our children. This is an ongoing process that begins at an early age and then changes as children grow and mature. In this regard, we (parents) are teachers and disciple-makers, primarily through our example, rather than our words.

When referring to Christian discipleship, we need to think in terms of relationship, rather than merely an equipping process. The discipleship relationship is best transmitted through the process of life-sharing that includes emotions, values, and experiences. For this to happen, we need to create a family atmosphere.

How do we do this? Family psychology tells us that every parent should be a nurturer and a disciplinarian. A great parent must spiritually and emotionally nourish children. And this nourishment should be given with words of affection, admiration, security, and the declaration of life, hope and blessing. Children must know that the parents are accessible and conscious of their spiritual and emotional needs. Great parenting also includes lots of "play" time. I'm referring to sharing informal settings where it's possible to know and be known. Going to the park, having a picnic, or watching a movie are great examples of this informal "fun" atmosphere. These are ways to strengthen relationships and grow in everyday life.

Finally, great parenting should correct, and challenge attitudes so that the character of Christ shines through. This is only possible if parents have first won the hearts of their children. The only correction that makes a lasting impact is also accompanied by love (1 Corinthians 8:1).

I once heard that you have to raise children like disciples because they will grow and surpass their teacher. The reality is that children grow, leave home, but will always be impacted by the relationships with their parents. What kind of relationships do you have with your disciples? [36]

The Church as family fulfills God's plan to make disciples and send them out to a lost and hurting world. Individual disciples must function as a community, the family of God.[37]

TRUTH TELLING IN COMMUNITY

Paul had Christian community in mind when he wrote to the house church in Ephesus, "Instead, speaking the truth in love, we will in all things grow up into him who is the Head, that is, Christ. From him the whole body, joined and held together by every supporting ligament, grows and builds itself up in love, as each part does its work" (Ephesians 4:15-16). Supernatural healing takes place when wounded healers (those who have received God's comfort) speak God's truth to other group members in a humble, sensitive way. People need to first warm up to the small group before transformation happens. Wise leaders encourage group members to share honestly and to pray for one another to experience restoration and healing.

When Ted came to the cell group, everything appeared normal. After the lesson on forgiveness from 1 Peter 4:8, however, his need for transformation surfaced. He shared his deep resentment toward a pastor whom he felt had raped his daughter. Ted had been clinging to his bitterness toward this pastor, which left him joyless and enslaved. That night the word of God reached deep into his soul, and Ted realized he needed to be set free from his bitterness, both for his own sake and in order to please Jesus Christ. During the prayer time, Ted confessed his bitterness, and the group members prayed for him to experience inner transformation. Group members spoke into Ted's life, sharing their own battles with unforgiveness and God's supernatural healing. God began the process of freeing Ted that night from his bitterness and resentment, and he left the meeting filled with joy and peace.

The church is a hospital. Everyone has been hurt. No one escapes the pain of this world, and no one will experience complete healing until the next life. The best we can do is fulfill our roles as wounded healers, offering to others the same comfort that we also have received.

This is why I exhort leaders not to jump too quickly into Bible study. I encourage them to spend plenty of time on prayer requests, particular needs during the week, ice-breaker questions, or any other open-ended opportunity for people to share deeply, receive prayer, and allow other wounded healers to speak words of encouragement. We become disciples as we share in life's journey and allow others to speak the truth in love. Larry Crabb affirms this truth saying,

> Ordinary people have the power to change other people's lives. . . the power is found in connection, that profound meeting when the truest part of one's soul meets the emptiest recesses in another and finds something there, when life passes from one to the other. When that happens, the giver is left more full than before and the receiver less terrified, eventually eager, to experience even deeper, more mutual connection. [38]

Ministering to ordinary hurting people through small group ministry was the driving force behind the eighteenth century Methodist movement that transformed England. John Wesley, the founder of the Methodist movement, understood the need for group members to hold each other accountable through transparent sharing. Each small group member was expected to "speak freely and plainly about every subject for [from] their own temptations to plans for establishing a new cottage meeting or visiting the distressed." [39]

Many believe that the Methodist small groups were instrumental in saving eighteenth century England from anarchy and disaster (drunkenness and lawlessness was at an all-time high in England immediately before the Methodist revival). The Methodist groups were not merely Bible studies, although Wesley encouraged all those around him to study the Bible and doctrine. Rather, the emphasis was on practicing the one-anothers of the scriptures and promoting holiness and spirituality through Christian community. Wesley wrote, "You wish to serve God and to go heaven? Remember that you cannot serve him alone. You must therefore find companions, or make them; the Bible knows nothing of solitary religion." [40]

We in the twenty-first century church need to apply the lessons of community and discipleship that were the cornerstone to the Methodist revival in the eighteenth century. Wesley realized that people transformation happened in life-giving small groups. After all, Wesley didn't originate the small group discipleship strategy. Jesus did.

Chapter Four

DISCIPLESHIP THROUGH THE PRIESTHOOD OF ALL BELIEVERS

I recently spoke to a group of leaders in an older denomination about cell ministry. Several expressed disbelief when I talked about developing lay people in home groups. The potential division it might cause dismayed them. Their view of the church was closely tied with their buildings.

During one of the breaks, a pastor approached me to ask about cell ministry and for me to recommend a book that might help in starting new groups. I asked him what he was planning on doing, and he told me he planned on starting four groups in the homes of four different lay people. I was impressed with his idea, but as he explained more, my attitude quickly changed.

He said that each of these four groups would only meet once every three months and that he, the pastor, would lead each group! In the conversation it became clear that he didn't trust the lay people to facilitate groups. He was convinced that he, the minister, was the only one who could lead these groups, even if they only met four times per year!

Some pastors, like the one mentioned above, believe that they are responsible to do the work of the ministry, rather than preparing lay people to do it. They are not willing to give away their authority to others, even though Ephesians 4:11-12 is crystal clear that the main role of the pastor/teacher is to prepare lay people to do the work of the ministry.

On many occasions I've heard pastors talk about the dangers of allowing lay leaders to do the work of the ministry through cell groups. Sadly, the focus is always on the disastrous consequences, rather than the potential for discipleship growth. We can learn a lot from Jesus and the apostles who trusted the Holy Spirit to guide and direct new leadership.[41] Bill Hull, pastor and prolific author on discipleship, writes, "The priesthood of the believer implies that Christians have the authority and responsibility to minister for Christ as the priesthood traditionally did. If you join the priesthood of the believer with the common believer's call to ministry, you have the reasons for teaching that every Christian is called to Christian service." [42] God said through Moses, "Let my people go." Just as it was true back then, it's equally true today. God wants his people set free. He wants them to learn to be disciples as they minister to others.

EVERYONE A MINISTER

The priesthood of all believers dates back to biblical times. John the apostle wrote, "To him who loves us and has freed us from our sins by his blood, and has made us to be a kingdom and priests to serve his God and Father—to him be glory and power for ever and ever!" (Revelation 1:5-6)

Early Christianity viewed each house church member as a minister. Ministry through the gifts of the Spirit flowed naturally in the home environment, and leadership development was simple and dynamic. Leadership was based on God-given gifts, rather than a stiff, liturgical hierarchy. The priesthood of all believers was the norm in the early Church, and for this reason the early Church spread rapidly. Gilbert Bilezikian writes,

> In a few decades, the early church movement spread like wildfire through the ancient world. One of the secrets for this rapid expansion was total lay involvement in the ministries of the local churches . . . The book of Acts and most of the New Testament letters are permeated with the euphoria and the vitality of churches where everyone was involved in body life and ministry. Under normal circumstances, therefore, the apostle Paul was more interested in encouraging Christian folks to minister to each other and together than in setting up orders of hierarchy for their governance. [43]

As the Church moved beyond the first century, the growing authority of the bishop concentrated more and more power in the hands of centralized authority figures responsible for larger and larger groups of believers.[44] The plurality and equality of leadership gave way to a hierarchical arrangement with bishops becoming the central figure followed by the presbyters (who later became priests) and deacons.

As the years passed, the Church became more and more hierarchical. People couldn't go directly to God but needed to access God through the priests. Only certain people had access to the Bible. Luther caused a rift within the structured Catholic church by establishing the preaching of the word as the central place in church life.

Luther exposed the abuses of the Church by teaching the Bible and then translating it into the German language, so that each believer could judge for himself what was right and wrong. One of the key doctrines that Luther brought back was the *priesthood of the believer*, which affirmed that each believer could read the Bible, understand scripture's plain meaning, had equal access to God, and was expected to serve and minister to the greater body of Christ. The *priesthood of the believer* taught that all Christians were priests, which stood in complete opposition to the concept of a spiritual aristocracy or hierarchy within Christianity.

Luther helped liberate the church doctrinally, but did little in the area of ecclesiology (study of church practices). He, along with Zwingli and the other reformers, could not fully encourage others to practice the *priesthood of all believers*. They needed the protection of the government and the stability of the entire state to embrace their reforms, and their success required that everyone in the state automatically become Protestants. In other words, there was very little choice about church involvement since the entire nation had to join the church. The *priesthood of all believers* had little practical application in the state-run church.

Some wanted to take the *priesthood of all believers* to its logical conclusion. They were called the "radical brethren" and believed that only those truly born again believers should come together to worship and receive adult baptism. These radical believers felt that each believing adult was a true minister, should have the right to form small groups, and exercise spiritual gifts within the small group. Summing up the situation, Nigel Wright says,

> It is important to stress that the real issue between Zwingli and the radical brethren was not baptism but the nature

of the church. Zwingli was out to reform the church but (as Luther had already conceded and as Calvin was to do) he accepted without question the concept of the sacral state which he had inherited and which had prevailed since the Edict of Milan in A.D. 311, when Christianity was officially tolerated, eventually to become the official religion of the Empire. [45]

Reformers like Luther, Zwingli, and Calvin made a huge break with church tradition and doctrine but the radical brethren took the reforms further. They wanted to make true disciples through a believer's church, rather than acting like everyone born in a particular geographical area were part of Christ's church, which would later be sorted out via predestination.

The radical reformation is closer to New Testament Christianity because it prioritizes the priesthood of each believer. Whatever a person's denominational tradition, we all need to be radical reformers! The radical reformation teaches the need to practice biblical doctrines in a way that emphasizes every person a minister and every believer a practicing disciple of Jesus Christ, just like the practice of the early Church.

The house churches of the first century expected each believer to minister in the house church setting. The cell church today, like the early church, is a call for radical reformation. It's a return to New Testament Christianity and to embrace the apostle's exhortation in the last book of the Bible, "To him who loves us and has freed us from our sins by his blood, and has made us to be a kingdom and priests to serve his God and Father—to him be glory and power for ever and ever! Amen" (Revelation 1:5-6).

ACTIVE PARTICIPATION

One important principle of the *priesthood of all believers* is involvement. In other words, all members of Christ's Church should be involved in using their gifts and talents.

Cell ministry stands against the idea that the official pastor or minister does most of the work, while the laity sits and listen—and perhaps engage in a few programs. The spectator emphasis in many churches undermines discipleship because only a few participate while many simply attend.

The situation is a lot like inactive fans at a football game who are cheering for the sweating players on the field. The players are doing all the work, while the fans just observe and clap. Elton Trueblood once said:

> All of us suffer from a terrible sickness in our churches. It is called Spectatoritis. We speak of the congregation as the audience. We are not the audience; we are the actors. . . . If we sincerely believe the Gospel, we have to believe that God has a vocation for each of us. The secret is participation, participation, participation. [46]

Participation is at the core of the cell. No one sits in the back seat. Chairs are not arranged in rows. As people share their stories, ask for prayer, and minister to one another, they are transformed in the process. They become the ministers and grow as Christ's disciples. The best cell leaders, in fact, are facilitators. The word *facilitate* means *to make easy*, and the best facilitators make it easy for others to participate. They unwrap the gifts and talents of those in the group. The best facilitators, in fact, only talk thirty percent of the time and encourage those in the group to speak the remaining seventy percent. Talking, of course, is only one aspect of cell life. Participation is far broader and involves active engagement in each part of the cell group.

I often tell those in my seminars that the best-kept secret of pastoral ministry is that the pastor grows more than those in the congregation. Why? Because the pastor matures as he depends on God to preach, counsel, visit the sick, prepare for a funeral, or marry a new couple. Discipleship, in other words, takes place as the pastor depends on God for every aspect of pastoral ministry. If pastors could better grasp that growth comes through participation, they would do a lot more to get people actively involved in ministry, and I believe that the New Testament pattern of house to house ministry is the best option.

This is one main reason why Jesus chose the small group atmosphere to impart knowledge to his own disciples. Christ wanted the information to be disseminated into the lives of his disciples, so as he journeyed with them each day for three years, he not only taught them, but asked them to interact with and apply his teachings. Sometimes Jesus would allow them to make mistakes in order to teach them important lessons and offer practical application of his teachings. Jesus, for example, allowed Peter to walk to him on the water. Jesus knew he would sink in the process but that valuable lessons would also be learned (Matthew 14:29). The disciples tried to cast out a demon and could not, but later Jesus gave them important instructions about what to do next time (Mark 9:18). The disciples were convinced that Christ would establish his kingdom right there and then, but Jesus taught them about their invisible guide, the Holy Spirit (Acts 1:7-8). Christ's method of discipleship was a constant interaction between hearing, doing, failing, learning, and then teaching new lessons. Christ not only practiced this methodology with his disciples, but those same disciples formed house churches that continued the process of group participation.

Effective cells and cell leaders make disciples in the same way Jesus made them. They encourage everyone to participate, knowing that discipleship happens when everyone is practicing the priesthood of all believers. The cell is small enough to mobilize each person. Participation in a group larger than fifteen can cause fear and resistance. But when the group is small and intimate, people still feel the face-to-face involvement of each person.

WALKING ON WATER

Roland Allen (1868-1947), an Anglican minister and missionary to China, noticed God's work was often hindered through not trusting the Holy Spirit to work through ordinary people. He began to study the life of the apostle Paul and realized that Paul developed lay people quickly and effectively because he trusted the Holy Spirit's work in his converts. Allen writes, "Paul had such faith in Christ and the Holy Spirit indwelling in the church that he did not shrink from risks. Even when the Galatians fell prey to the Judaizer's legalism, we don't sense that Paul tried to change his method of church planting." [47] Paul, in other words, understood the potential for error, but he also knew that inactivity wasn't the answer. Paul knew that starting house churches where people would experience face-to-face ministry and then trusting the Holy Spirit through each person was essential in making disciples who made disciples.

If we fail to allow the Holy Spirit to energize people, we do them a grave disservice. We are actually hindering the person from being all God wants him or her to be. Allowing people to participate actively in God's work is risky, and yes, we will not always be able to control what happens. But this is the very essence of trusting the Holy Spirit to work deeply within people, even if it's messy. Roland Allen writes, "By spontaneous expansion I mean something which we cannot control. And if we cannot control it, we ought, as I think, to rejoice that we cannot control it. For if we cannot control it, it is because it is too great; not because it is too small for us. The great things of God are beyond our control." [48]

The apostle John reminded each house church member of the Holy Spirit's anointing. He said, "As for you, the anointing you received from him remains in you, and you do not need anyone to teach you. But as his anointing teaches you about all things and as that anointing is real, not counterfeit—just as it has taught you, remain in him" (1 John 2:27). Many churches hesitate to start cells because they're afraid that members might undermine the church or draw away disciples from the ministry. But the danger of stagnation carries far graver risks. The risk of not releasing the lay people is inactivity, lack of growth, and an atrophied church. It's the opposite of making disciples who make disciples. Risk taking is normal and it's the way people mature and grow. Listen to Henry Cloud and John Townsend write about risk-taking in their best-selling book, *Boundaries:*

> The sin God rebukes is not trying and failing, but failing to try. Trying, failing, and trying again is called learning. Failing to try will have no good result; evil will triumph. God expresses his opinion toward passivity in Hebrews 10:38-39: "But my righteous one will live by faith. And if he shrinks back, I will not be pleased with him." . . . Passive shrinking back is intolerable to God, and when we understand how destructive it is to the soul, we can see why God does not tolerate it. [49]

Cell members and leaders grow to become like Jesus as they step out and exercise their faith. Without doing so, the person will not grow to his or her full potential. Trying and failing is how we learn and grow and become mature. The fear of error has caused many churches to smother the work of the laity through endless requirements and layers of organization. Churches and mission agencies have done this for years.

What does this mean practically? It means mobilizing each cell member to participate—without forcing people against their will. One member might lead the prayer time, another lead worship, another guide the ice-breaker, while someone else leads the outreach time. The best cells have leadership teams who don't depend on one leader to always facilitate the lesson. I was in one cell church which viewed cell leaders as coaches of those who led the lesson time. In other words, the cell leader was always present in the cell but different members rotated in actually leading the cell lesson. The cell leader would offer feedback and encouragement. The cell groups in this particular church also rotated hosts, so that everyone had the opportunity of opening their home to the group. I could feel the health because I sensed that disciples were being formed as each person participated.

Some cell churches also encourage their leaders to perform pastoral duties in the larger gatherings. The cell leaders might baptize the new converts, for example. [50] Other churches ask lay leaders to serve communion or rotate in the Sunday preaching. Cell members might help with ushering, outreaches, or mission events. Participation grows disciples. Sitting in a pew and hearing doctrine is important, but it doesn't mold active disciples like Jesus commanded.

PLAYING YOUR PART

Paul writes about the body of Christ to house churches that were meeting in Corinth (1 Corinthians 12-14), Rome (Romans 12) and Ephesus (Ephesians 4). Those reading his letters were in relationship with each other and ministering together. Paul makes it clear that each person in the body of Christ had an important role to play. Notice what he said to the house churches in Corinth:

> Now the body is not made up of one part but of many. If the foot should say, "Because I am not a hand, I do not belong to the body," it would not for that reason cease to be part of the body. And if the ear should say, "Because I am not an eye, I do not belong to the body," it would not for that reason cease to be part of the body. If the whole body were an eye, where would the sense of hearing be? If the whole body were an ear, where would the sense of smell be? But in fact God has arranged the parts in the body, every one of them, just as he wanted them to be. If they were all one part, where would the body be? As it is, there are many parts, but one body. . . . If one part suffers, every part suffers with it; if one part is honored, every part rejoices with it. Now you are the body of Christ, and each one of you is a part of it (1 Corinthians 12:12-28).

In the cell group, each person plays an essential role. In fact, those who seemingly have a more visible role are not more important. The parts that are unseen are given special honor. The body needs each other to be healthy and whole. The goal is for everyone to participate, discover their gifts, and minister to others. The teaching that the church is the body of Christ is to remind the Church that every believer is valuable and essential and needs to exercise his or her gifts. [51]

God sets each of us in his supernatural, organic body according to the gifts of the Spirit (1 Corinthians 12-14). In all three of the major passages in which Paul talks about the body of Christ, he defines each member's part in the body by their corresponding gifts (Ephesians 4; Romans 12; 1 Corinthians 12-14). In fact, when Paul talks about the Church as the body of Christ, the implication is that the believers were actively participating. They had the opportunity to interact among themselves as they met in house churches. They grew together as disciples as they exercised their spiritual gifts and ministered to one another.

Gift use in the Early Church

The ministry in the early house churches was fluid and dynamic. Members were encouraged to experience their spiritual gifts for the common good of the body, and leaders operated as gifted men and women (Romans 12:6-8; 1 Corinthians 12:8-10, 27-28). Dependence on the Spirit of God through the gifts of the Spirit shaped the direction of the early Church. The spiritual gifts mentioned in 1 Corinthians 12-14, Romans 12:3-8, Ephesians 4:7-12, and 1 Peter 4:8-11 were written to those participating in house churches. Everyone participated in the building up of Christ's body. [52]

Paul expected church leadership to develop according to spiritual giftedness and that ultimately the Holy Spirit would set each member in the body according to his will and purpose (1 Corinthians 12:11). The early church believed that the Spirit was given to all believers and was actively working through each member (Romans 12:11; 1 Corinthians 2:4, 12:7; 12-13; Galatians 3:5; 5:18, 22; 1 Thessalonians 5:19-21). [53]

God did gift certain individuals to lead his Church as we can see in Ephesians 4:7-12. Many have called this the five-fold ministry, although it's probably more accurate to call it the four-fold ministry, since pastor-teacher is often considered one role. Gifted leaders included:

- Apostles: The twelve (Luke 6:13-16), plus Matthias (Acts 1:24-26), Paul (Galatians 1:1), Barnabas (Acts 14:14), Andronicus and Junias (Romans 16:7)
- Prophets: The company from Jerusalem (Acts 11:27-28), Agabus (Acts 21:10-11), Judas and Silas (Acts 15:32) and the daughters of Philip (Acts 21:9)
- Evangelists: Philip's daughters (Acts 21:9)
- Pastor-teachers (1 Timothy 3:1-3, 5:17; Titus 1:5, 7, 9)

The gifted leaders mentioned in Ephesians were specifically equipped to prepare the body of Christ to minister more effectively. In other words, God equipped these men and women to mobilize the church for service. [54]

Paul's main point in Ephesians is equipping the saints for ministry. The specific purpose of gifted men and women is to equip the Church for growth and expansion. The focus is not on the gifted person, but on his or her ministry to equip the body of Christ so that the body of Christ would be built up and mobilized for service. Whatever gift God distributes to a particular person, his or her main role is to equip God's people to become better disciples of Jesus Christ through participatory ministry.

Paul also mentions some twenty gifts (not just four or five) and wants his readers to know that each house church member needed to minister according to his or her giftedness (1 Corinthians 12-14; Romans 12; Ephesians 4:11-12; 1 Peter 4:8-11). And whether recognized formally or not, each member had an important part to play in the body of Christ (1 Corinthians 12:12-26). The spiritual gifts were to build up the body of Christ in unity and maturity.

Gift use in the Cell Group

Today, more than ever, we need to get back to the small group as the primary place to exercise spiritual gifts. It is the most natural atmosphere for everyone to participate and grow as disciples. It is also the most spontaneous and biblical place for the discovery of our spiritual gifts, which enhances ministry and the priesthood of all believers. In the loving atmosphere of a home group, especially where the gifts are working and where the Holy Spirit is operating, people grow in ministry and learn how to serve others.

Effective cell leaders encourage everyone in the cell to use their particular gifts, so the body might be edified and non-Christians might be won to Christ. The place to start is to remind the members that each one has at least one gift. 1 Peter 4:10 tells us that ". . . one should use whatever gift he has received to serve others, faithfully administrating God's grace in its various forms." As group members discover and exercise their spiritual gifts, they will grow in their faith and become more like Jesus.

If someone has the gift of prophesy, for example, there's an open door to use it. The person doesn't need to prophesy in a high-pitched shrill "prophesy" voice. Rather the person can speak to those present very naturally. Kirk regularly prophesies in the cell group, and he also encourages other people to step out and give their prophetic impressions. Kirk always starts his prophecies by saying, "I think the Holy Spirit is saying to me. . ." He then asks each member to discover for themselves whether his words conform to scripture. Kirk realizes that human beings can make mistakes—and that he's no exception. Kirk also realizes that all prophecy must have the goal of edifying the body (1 Corinthians 14:3).

The person with the gift of teaching might help clarify a difficult passage. The one who has the gift of teaching doesn't need to do all the teaching. Rather, he or she might give insight into a particular passage, helping to make the Bible clear and concise. She will also help others apply the teaching of scripture to their own lives.

Leo had the gift of teaching but never had the chance to use it, until he got involved in a cell group. Then the gift came alive. He was able to clarify a passage of scripture and make it understandable and applicable. He had been a member of a denominational church for most of his adult life but had mainly attended church and occasionally received visits from the pastor. But as Leo interacted face-to-face in a cell group, his teaching gift became crystal clear. Over time, Leo became the co-leader of the group.

Matt has the gift of pastor, but it lay dormant for years. The act of going to church and getting involved in programs just didn't interest him, and he avoided it. But in the cell group, he had a chance to share, minister, and use his gifts. He grew spiritually as he ministered to others, and it soon became apparent that he was the pastor of the group and felt responsible to gather the people, stay in touch with them, mobilize the outreach, and develop others in the group. Matt followed his giftedness and the body of Christ was built up. Matt also grew in his own walk with Jesus.

The person with the gift of mercy might visit a hurting cell member in the hospital and then mobilize others to visit that person. The believer with the gift of evangelism might feel compelled to invite friends and relatives or organize a cell outreach.

The person with the gift of exhortation will find someone who needs counseling. She might counsel hurting people after or before the cell meeting or during the week. This person will humbly offer counsel, not as a professional, but as a gifted member of the body of Christ. The gift will grow, as will the person, over time.

The person with the gift of apostleship will have a natural propensity to start new groups, but this person will not project himself above others, nor wear an *apostle Jim* name tag or pass out *apostle* business cards. Rather, he or she will serve the rest of Christ's body.

The cell group is also the natural place to use and develop talents. Debby, for example, loves to play the guitar. She also leads worship in the cell group on Thursday night. She diligently practices guitar, prints out song sheets, and leads the group in worship. Her talent for playing the guitar is empowered by her gift of leadership and prophecy. The pastor noticed her faithfulness to play guitar in the cell group and eventually asked her to play guitar in the worship band on Sunday morning.

Spiritual gifts are given for the good of the Church. Small groups are wonderful places to experiment with our *unknown* spiritual gifts, even risking failure, because we know that the small group will be forgiving of mistakes. If the person doesn't feel the freedom to fail, he or she won't grow as Christ's disciple.

Some people have tried to mobilize the gift ministry apart from a small-group setting (e.g., programs), but I believe it's far more fruitful to promote spiritual gifts through small-group ministry. In small groups, encouragement and accountability are more likely to occur spontaneously. This environment seems to be the natural place to grow disciples who are exercising their God-given gifts.

Gift Discovery through Relationships

The best way to discover spiritual gifts is in the context of relationship. Spiritual gift tests, while helping believers to think through the possibilities, are insufficient in themselves. Gift surveys do give a glimpse of how to perceive giftedness, but people can project into those questionnaires the gifts they *want* to have, rather than affirming the gifts they actually have. [55] The more people develop relationships in the context of a group, the better idea they will have concerning their own spiritual giftedness—always remembering that gifts function in the context of relationships. I encourage believers to read material, take one or two gift tests, step out in the exercise of potential spiritual gifts and then seek confirmation from others. Were people edified? Was Christ glorified? When trust is high, members feel like they can experiment with a variety of gifts, and they don't feel thwarted.

In the larger worship service, naturally experimenting with the gifts rarely happens because a larger audience demands a certain level of performance. Risk-taking is not encouraged in such an environment, nor should it be. The larger wing of the church is often the least effective place to exercise spiritual gifts because only a few believers can actually exercise their gifts in the large-group atmosphere. How many can lead worship? How many can preach? How many can usher? In reality, ministries involved with the celebration wing of the church are limited. Yet, in the safety of the small group and with the encouragement of the group leader, experimentation can happen, and the Holy Spirit will bless.

Look for Confirmation

Once the group becomes comfortable with each other and more knowledgeable about spiritual gifts, the leader can encourage them to confirm in each other their spiritual gifts in the small-group time. What do people confirm in you? If they notice your capacity to clarify the meaning of scripture, you may have the gift of teaching. My wife's gift of counseling (exhortation) has been confirmed over and over in the small-group environment. The gifts were given for the edification of the body of Christ, and when you edify someone with your gift, others will let you know.

It's important to remember that often a particular gift springs up in the presence of a particular need: a person with emotional difficulties, a demon-possessed person, a non-Christian with serious questions. In the presence of such needs, the Holy Spirit might endow you with a gifting that you *didn't* know you had (and perhaps, you didn't have it until that moment!). Although I believe that each believer has at least one more or less permanent gift, the Holy Spirit can bestow special gifts in the presence of particular needs.

Gift discovery takes place in the process of serving one another, caring for one another and living the life of the body. When you find that God *consistently* blesses your efforts in a certain area, you can confidently conclude that you have that particular gift.

Some churches magnify just one or two gifts, to the exclusion of others. Some have called this process *gift colonization*. If the pastor is a gifted evangelist with regular campaigns, there may be a strong tendency to organize the entire church around evangelism. The other gifts of the Holy Spirit may be less likely to be manifested in the church because like-minded people will either stay or leave, depending on whether or not they like the pastor.

Great group facilitators, on the other hand, allow for more diversity. The leader needs to be open to allow people to experiment with gifts that are different from his or her own gift mix—as long as the use of that gift edifies the rest of the group. As the group leader gives members more liberty to exercise their gifts, the members will experience a new responsibility and will consequently feel more committed to the church.

Check your Desire Level

One of the main secrets behind discovering spiritual giftedness is trying to determine your "desire level" to operate in a particular gift. Exercising a gift should not be a chore—it should be enjoyed. You should experience a high degree of passion and desire when exercising your spiritual gifts. I like to ask those trying to identify spiritual giftedness:

> Do you like explaining biblical truth? Perhaps you have the gift of teaching. Do you enjoy praying for people in the group, and when you do, do you see them healed? Perhaps you have the gift of healing. Do you love to bring refreshments and organize group events? Perhaps you have the gift of helps or administration. Are you drawn to visit cell members who are having problems? Perhaps you have the gift of mercy.

Joy, excitement and fulfillment should accompany the exercise of spiritual gifts. Greg Ogden writes in *The New Reformation:* "The central clue to discovering our spiritual gifts is to get in touch with the spheres of service that produce a flow of inner joy, excitement and energy." [56] When it feels heavy and burdensome to exercise a spiritual gift, it might be because no such gift exists—the person was simply trying to fulfill in the flesh what only the Holy Spirit can do through his *charismata.*

YOU ARE NEEDED

Candice Millard, author of *The River of Doubt: Theodore Roosevelt's Darkest Journey,* skillfully pieces together the true story of Roosevelt's trek down the *River of Doubt,* an unexplored one thousand-mile river in the deep Amazonian rainforest. Roosevelt and his team joined forces with Brazil's most famous explorer, Candido Rondon. Before it was over, the explorers faced deadly rapids, Indian attacks, disease, starvation and a murderer within their own ranks. Writing to a friend later on, Roosevelt confessed, "The Brazilian wilderness stole away 10 years of my life." In fact, he never fully recovered his prior vigor and was troubled by recurring malaria until his death in 1919. Yet, the fact that the team mapped out an unknown Amazon tributary and lived to tell about it was so incredible that many naturalists of that day didn't believe it actually happened.

As I read the book, I was struck by the unity the team developed in order to survive. Every team member had to fulfill his role as they fought against the odds. Because of the dwindling food and poor initial planning, the team had to get rid of unnecessary luxuries and even separate from team members who were not fulfilling their duties. At one point when Roosevelt was seriously injured, he pleaded with the team to leave him behind to die in the jungle because he didn't want to be a burden to the rest of the group. The only way they survived, in fact, was each member pulling his weight and working together. As they did, they lived to tell about their incredible journey on the River of Doubt.

The Church is on a journey in a hostile environment, one that is diametrically opposed to its Christ-like organic nature. Every member of the body of Christ needs to be actively involved for the Church to overcome the world, flesh, and the devil. Each person must actively use his gift and minister in his God-given capacity. For far too long, the church has depended on one or two body parts to do the work of the ministry. Now Christ is calling his Church to actively make disciples who are making new disciples through cell ministry. This is the path to effectiveness and spiritual growth.

Chapter Five

DISCIPLESHIP THROUGH GROUP EVANGELISM

Here in Southern California we have amusement parks such as Disneyland, Knott's Berry Farm, and Magic Mountain. I've lived in this area most of my life, and at some point in the last fifty-seven years, I've experienced many of the exciting rides in each of these parks—including some of the most exhilarating roller coasters in the world.

The journey of the disciples with Jesus reminds me of a three-year roller coaster ride. They grew more like Jesus in the process, but it certainly wasn't easy. The disciples went from a career of fishing to following a miracle worker who opened blind eyes, multiplied loaves of bread, and raised dead people from the grave. They heard the best teaching from the perfect teacher—the God-man. And they were taught in an unsurpassed didactic setting that included hearing, doing, and application to real life experiences. One teaching that escaped them, however, was Christ's death and resurrection.

When Jesus died on the cross, it felt like the roller coaster had flown off the rails. It's hard to imagine how horrendous it must have felt for the disciples to watch Jesus suffer and die on the cross. They all forsook him and fled.

But the ride wasn't over. In three days, Jesus rose again. He appeared to them and their joy was overwhelming. They could see with their own eyes that Jesus was alive and even the brutal Roman cross couldn't keep him down. Christ had already breathed the Holy Spirit on them, and his strange parables began to make sense.

Now it was their turn to do radical things and turn the world upside down. Jesus told them to go into the entire world and make new disciples. They already knew what strategy to use because the Master had prepared them to go into the homes, get to know the householder, watch for divine appointments, and then stay in the same home until the city was reached.

They were ready to work but were very fearful. Then Pentecost happened. They were empowered. The Holy Spirit dominated their lives and they preached boldly. They established house churches, just like Jesus had taught them.

They proclaimed the good news and let the world know Jesus lived by their own transformed lives. When persecuted, they blessed and prayed for their enemies. They allowed the Holy Spirit to take care of the rest. Yet the entire experience was ordained by God to grow them and make them more like Jesus.

And the early church grew and multiplied. As Jesus transformed people, they behaved differently within their family relationships. Husbands loved wives, slaves were treated with dignity, and married partners submitted to one another. Friends and neighbors were drawn to this new transformed community. The Christian movement attracted people because of the

Christians' behavior toward one another and toward those outside the church. People could see the changes up close as community life was lived out in the open.

Growth in those early house churches was organic and natural. Evangelistic expansion was built into the way of life of the church, and in this same organic setting, church members became disciples. We can learn lots from the early house church movement—especially how to create an environment for discipling where evangelism naturally happens.

GIVING COMMUNITY AWAY

Paul the apostle summarizes growth through evangelism when writing to a house church in the first century, "I pray that you may be active in sharing your faith, so that you will have a full understanding of every good thing we have in Christ" (Philemon verse 6). As this house church in Colossae shared their faith, they grew in their relationship with Jesus Christ and became strong disciples as a result.

Many in the western world have learned to share their faith individually, but we haven't been as successful in practicing group evangelism. Yet, group evangelism is at the heart of New Testament evangelism.

One of the first barriers to overcome is the underlying assumption that evangelistic outreach weakens community. Normally group members love community and have tasted its transforming power. They just don't believe that community and evangelism go together. Research and experience, however, show that better, more biblical community develops when a cell reaches out to non-Christians. The process of evangelizing, in fact, strengthens the bonds of community. When a new person comes to the group, members develop close bonds as they minister to the newcomer.

When the group only focuses on fellowship, it is missing an important aspect of spiritual growth and failing to take the group members to the next level of discipleship. The very process of cell evangelism brings spiritual growth, not just when someone comes to the group or receives Jesus. I encourage cell groups, therefore, to pray for non-Christians each week and plan ways to reach out, even if those evangelistic efforts don't bring much fruit.

When a small group has a common evangelistic objective, it starts working together to accomplish the outreach goal. This mutual vision creates a unity and camaraderie. Everyone gets involved—from the person who invites the guests to the one who provides refreshments to the one who leads the discussion. The team plans, strategizes, and finds new contacts together.

The cry of the lost drives cells to share their rich community rather than hoarding it among themselves. When multiplication takes place, new groups are available for lost people to receive Christ-like community. The friendship and love develops in the process. Today's broken society desperately needs a loving family. How will people find it unless small groups are living in community and willing to spread it?

STEPPING OUT AS FRIENDS

God is the one who converts, but he expects us to do our part. I'll never forget doing a cell seminar in Ireland in 2007 with Laurence Singlehurst, bestselling author on evangelism and cell church pioneer in the UK. He asked people from the audience to come forward and then asked them to form a small group in front of everyone. He posed as the leader of the group and asked each one whom they were praying for and what they were doing to reach out (this was in front of about eight hundred people!). I don't remember the responses, but everyone in the audience was listening intently, and Singlehurst succeeded in demonstrating how to mobilize a cell group to reach out.

Kim and Kim Cole are shining examples of praying for the lost, reaching out to their non-Christian neighbors, and mobilizing their cell to minister to others. Kim Cole, the wife, told me that her church's emphasis on friendship evangelism not only transformed their own lives but also the members of the cell group.

Kim was born and raised in York, PA and accepted Jesus at York Alliance Church when she was fourteen years old. She experienced great teaching, friendships, and memories during her years at the church. Yet she also realized that during those years, York Alliance Church concentrated primarily on church-based programs. When York Alliance started emphasizing cell ministry in 2001, she and her husband, Kim, recognized that God was challenging them to reach their own neighborhood for Jesus.

She, along with the other cell members, began developing relationships with close friends and neighbors. She understood that she needed to open up her own life to those around her. She told me, "It's very scary to live life in the open. I was not accustomed to being real to my neighbors." On one occasion she made home-made ice-cream in the front yard and invited neighbors to join in. The neighbors began to get to know the Coles as they interacted around fun things. Kim told me that those in her neighborhood were from English and Irish descent and took great pride in their homes. She discovered that the best way to enter their worlds was to ask for help.

So she took a leap of faith and asked her neighbor, Crystal, who lived two doors down, if she could borrow a pot. Kim and Crystal talked at the doorstep and began developing a relationship. Crystal and her husband, Todd, were already going to a church, but the church didn't preach the gospel, and Crystal and Todd were not believers. As the relationship deepened, Kim eventually invited them to their life group. Crystal and Todd began attending the life group and also the Sunday worship service at York Alliance Church. Kim told me that she nearly lost them when they came to the church and read in the bulletin, "Invite your unsaved friend to the upcoming event." Crystal turned to Kim and said, "Is this what you think of me." Kim apologized, saying, "We really love you and just wanted you to come."

Crystal knew that Kim had something she needed, so she kept on coming back to the life group, wanting to experience something more. Crystal asked the hard questions, and Kim grew in the process of depending on God to give answers. Kim said to me, "I grew as much as Crystal during that time period." Crystal and Todd eventually received Jesus, got involved in the cell group, and made their way through the discipleship equipping (discussed in chapter 8). They eventually became life group leaders and continued the process of friendship evangelism.

The fruit of Kim's outreach and Crystal and Todd's subsequent conversion is a wonderful testimony. Kim and Kim Cole grew and matured in their relationship with Jesus in the process of reaching Crystal and Todd. Paul's words to the Colossae house church is worth repeating, "I pray that you may be active in sharing your faith, so that you will have a full understanding of every good thing we have in Christ" (Philemon verse 6). It's doubtful that we can know every good thing within us without giving those treasures out to others.

Kim and Kim Cole are exceptional. They've multiplied their own group some six times and have won many neighbors to Jesus. Their example has inspired the entire church. But we can't just depend on one or two people, like Kim and Kim Cole. Each member of the cell needs to do his or her part in relational outreach.

Developing relationships with non-Christians is not easy. It stretches our faith and stirs us to depend on God. We grow in the process. Often, relationships with non-Christians are developed in the context of something else. Coaching softball, going to one particular hairdresser, joining the volunteer board at the home association, or getting involved in a special interest group are among the many ways to build relationships. Developing business colleagues, sport associates, special interests and hobby associates are other ways to broaden your friendship base.

Communities are eager for volunteers to serve in social action programs, whether it is daycare, counseling, outreach to the homeless, or some other program. In every community there is an opportunity to share love and Christian values in a positive way. You can join a parent/teacher association, neighborhood watch, or one of the many other committees and organizations that make up the local community.

We've been getting to know our neighbors since returning from Ecuador in 2001. We invited them over for meals, asked if they had particular prayer requests, and brought them baked goods during the holidays. We developed a relationship with them, and we grew in the process of getting to know them.

When we invited them to join our home group, the husband said, "We can't make it on Tuesday night, but our youngest daughter would like you to baptize her." I said, "I'd be thrilled to do that. However, I'd like to take her and you through some discipleship material in preparation for baptism." I began to take the entire family through the first book of our discipleship equipping process, *Live*.

The first lesson was about knowing God, and each of them prayed the sinner's prayer as part of the lesson. We then continued to go through the book, in a relaxed, relational setting in their own home. I had the privilege of baptizing their daughter, yet the process has not stopped there, and the journey of discipleship continues.

The best cell facilitators, in fact, remind those in the group to develop relationships with non-Christians and then plan cell outreach activities. I remember speaking in an Assembly of God church in Vero Beach in which the cell groups were actively reaching out and encouraging their members to develop relationships with non-Christians. I heard many testimonies of the power of cell outreach. I soon learned that the lead pastor not only talked about evangelism but regularly hung out at the local restaurant with the sole purpose of getting to know non-Christians. He lived what he wanted others to follow and the cells in that church bore much fruit. Evangelism was a natural part of his own life and his zeal spread throughout the entire church.

Relational evangelism works best when the group is praying. I entered one host home and saw a mini-white board in the living room. The leader told me the cell group had bought the white board for the sole purpose of writing down names of non-Christians and then praying evangelistically for them. I noticed that several names were crossed off the list. The leader explained that God was miraculously answering prayer. Group members grew in their faith as they saw God answer prayer and were encouraged to keep praying and witnessing.

Not all members are excited to reach out. Some abhor the idea. I'll never forget the resistance I faced from a group member who said, "I came to this group for fellowship, not evangelism. I want to get to know people—not invite new ones to the group." I knew that our community would grow inward and stagnate unless we as a group made a concerted effort to reach out. I took the couple aside after the next meeting and told them that our group had the dual focus of community and outreach and that cell outreach was essential in the disciple-making process. Thankfully they accepted my exhortation, stayed in the group, and even reached out in their own neighborhood.

FISHING IN NEW TESTAMENT TIMES

As a teenager, I used to fish each year in Ensenada, Mexico. My family would camp at Estero Beach, and I would find my favorite spot on a rock near the entrance. I remember casting out my reel with two hooks and bringing in two decent size bass. The disciples, however, fished differently. They fished with nets rather than poles. Mark says:

> As Jesus walked beside the Sea of Galilee, he saw Simon and his brother Andrew casting a net into the lake, for they were fishermen. "Come, follow me," Jesus said, "and I will make you fishers of men." At once they left their nets and followed him. When he had gone a little farther, he saw James, son of Zebedee, and his brother John in a boat, preparing their nets (Mark 1:16-20).

When the disciples cast out their nets, they did it as a group and depended on each other to haul in the catch. When Jesus told them that he would make them fishers of men, he was also thinking about net fishing. Jesus, in fact, never sent the disciples out alone—only in teams. He wanted his disciples to live out the gospel before others so that the unbelievers might see their changed lives and believe in him.

Group evangelism takes the pressure off one person, and gives everyone the opportunity to exercise their faith and become disciples in the process. It's not the experience of one person doing the work of the ministry. Rather it's a shared experience. Everyone has a part to play. It's not the preacher's job. Success doesn't depend on the evangelist. In fact, there's a good chance the visitor will show up because of the quiet witness of one of the silent ones in the group. Wise cell leaders understand this and empower everyone in the group to do their part.

When the entire group sponsors an outreach activity (e.g., special film, barbeque, tea party, or something as fancy as a paint ball party) each person has a job. Dale Galloway, early pioneer of cell church ministry in the U.S., writes, "Once the list [of invitees] is built, the team begins to pray the prospect list, then to work it—making phone calls and home visitations. This responsibility can be shared with others in the small group." [57]

As we saw in the last chapter, personal involvement matures people as each becomes a priest of the living God. God uses large group evangelism, like campaigns and concerts, but the danger is a few people doing the lion's share of the work, while the rest just watch and stagnate. In cell group evangelism, there's the shared responsibility, which is critical for growth in discipleship. God desires that each member is using his or her muscles to reach out.

I spoke at a cell conference in Sydney, Australia, and the associate pastor of the host church, Michael, was very excited about cell evangelism. He joined the staff because of the evangelism potential through cell ministry. He previously was on staff at a large megachurch in which each person was instructed to tell others to come to the larger service so that the preacher could get them saved. Michael disagreed. He believed that each person was a minister and needed to be reaching out and evangelizing. He left that church because he believed that cell evangelism not only was more effective but also grew disciples in the process. The cells at the host church were robust and passionate about spreading the gospel message across the entire city. Pastor Michael played an important role in casting the evangelistic vision.

BELONGING AND THEN BELIEVING

My last name "Comiskey" is of Irish descent, so when we as a family visited Ireland in 2007, we were eager to explore the area. By far the greatest experience of the trip for me was to see where Saint Patrick ministered and to understand the impact Patrick had on Ireland. Saint Patrick combined discipleship with evangelism, and his relational strategy started a movement that changed the world.

In the fifth century A.D., when Patrick was about fourteen, he was captured by Irish raiders and taken as a slave to Ireland, where he lived for six years before escaping and returning to his family in England. God saved Patrick, raised him up to become a bishop in the church, and then called him to go back to Ireland as a missionary. Patrick's ministry was so effective that not only was most of Ireland converted, but God used the church in Ireland to send missionaries around the world.

Patrick's model of reaching out to others was highly relational, hospitable, and community-oriented. Patrick and his followers modeled what they wanted others to follow. They lived life in community, but this was never an end in itself. They never lost sight of giving their community away. Patrick and his followers would move into a pagan area, set up shop as a team, and become a part of the community. They tried to make the church accessible. They took seriously the passage in the book of Psalms that says, "Taste and see that the LORD is good; blessed is the man who takes refuge in him" (34:8). Patrick believed that the truth is first caught and then taught.

Saint Patrick's Celtic movement relied on Christ's own evangelistic strategy in John 17 where he tells the disciples that the world would know and believe by their unity. In fact, Patrick's bands of believers talked a lot about the love and unity within the Trinity and used the three-sided shamrock to explain the Trinity. The evangelistic bands knew their own lives needed to reflect God's character if they were going to win the unreached Irish.

Patrick taught that belonging comes before believing. They invited seekers to join their community and participate within it. Those who entered the group saw transformed lives, love in action, and how disciples were supposed to act. The seekers were then invited to become Christ's disciples. As a result of this strategy, many received Jesus, new groups multiplied, and missionary bands infiltrated unreached areas. The discipleship and the outreach were intimately connected together.

Saint Patrick started a movement, and he did it by developing relationships with the people and engaging their imagination by using symbols they understood. Many have made comparisons with Saint Patrick's ministry and our own current situation. Like the civilization in Saint Patrick's Day, people today are hungry for relationships. They want to taste Christ in their midst, become involved in a community, and then naturally grow in their relationship with Christ.

Actually, what Patrick accomplished in his day was very similar to evangelism in the early church, where neighbors could see and hear what was happening in the house churches. The unbelievers wanted change, became believers, and then grew naturally as disciples as they participated in a new community. People saved in those house churches were immediately known to the rest of the members, became part of a new family, were able to exercise their gifts and talents, and ultimately grew to become strong disciples of Jesus Christ.

Churches have spent countless hours trying to figure out how to connect "follow-up" with evangelism. The problem is that step one has been divorced from step two. The relational model offered by Saint Patrick and the early house churches brought people into the community, allowed them to see the change, and discipleship happened naturally in the process.

Loving relationships are attractive to the world. Jesus, in fact, told us that our love for one another would draw an unbelieving world to himself. As the church loves one another, people will be attracted to Jesus, become disciples, and then repeat the process of making more disciples.

NATURAL SHARING IN THE GROUP

I often tell the story of Dora, a lady in our cell group in Ecuador. Dora's parents were not believers. She often shared with the group her doubts about religion. People listened, loved her, and encouraged Dora to go directly to God with her doubts. One Tuesday evening in December, we showed part of the "Jesus" film at our home as part of a special Christmas outreach. Dora was with us, along with other seekers. Dora was accustomed to speaking her mind in the group and felt comfortable with everyone present. After showing the presentation, suddenly Dora cried out, "I'm confused." Everyone was shocked, but we simply loved Dora and cared for her as part of our family.

One week later, Dora received Jesus in our house. God used my wife Celyce to lead Dora to Jesus, but my wife was just one instrument. The entire cell group participated in Dora's conversion and follow-up. Each member of the group grew as disciples of Christ as much as Dora through being Dora's friend, witnessing to her, praying for her, and then welcoming her into the new family of God.

Dora matured over time, and we began to see her doubts fade away. Eventually, she was evangelizing others through prayer and connecting them to the cell. She began attending our larger Sunday celebration services, and I had the privilege of baptizing her in front of hundreds of people. She completed the discipleship equipping (more in chapter 8) and in the cell group we watched her grow and mature as she developed a deep relationship with God and others. Over time, she and her fiancé, Paul, began their own cell group, rescuing other "confused" people and drawing them to a new family of faith.

In the small group atmosphere, non-Christians can ask questions, share doubts, and talk about their own spiritual journey. Sharing openly gives unbelievers a new sense of hope as they realize that Christians have weaknesses and struggles too. More than an explanation, the "gospel" in the small group is seen and felt. The Holy Spirit is the one who convicts. [58] Dr. Peace, professor of evangelism for many years at Fuller Seminary, wrote the book, *Small Group Evangelism*. Peace believes the small group is the ideal place to evangelize and then to conserve the fruit of evangelism. Peace writes,

> . . . in a successful small group, love, acceptance and fellowship flow in unusual measure. This is the ideal situation in which to hear about the kingdom of God. In this context the "facts of the gospel" come through not as cold proposition but as living truths visible in the lives of others. In such an atmosphere a person is irresistibly drawn to Christ by his gracious presence. [59]

Those saved through this natural environment continue to grow through the relationships they've already established. They become disciples in the normal process of being part of the new family of God.

The reality is that often non-Christians stay away from churches because they have the mistaken idea that they have to be good enough to become Christians. They have known Christians who failed to live up to biblical standards and have seen phoniness in churches and the Christian mass media. Unbelievers long to know, see, and hear people who are on a journey, wrestling with God each day, not afraid to talk about marriage conflicts, and are willing to the share Christ's power to change people. These same non-Christians are refreshed when they go to a community of honest people who are willing to share their struggles with sin and their dependence on the living God. This type of authenticity often wins unbelievers to the Christian faith.

Cell members also come alive in their faith and grow as disciples in the presence of non-Christians. Paul the apostle was talking about a house church in 1 Corinthians 14:23ff. when he talks about an unbeliever entering the room. Paul says,

> So if the whole church comes together and everyone speaks in tongues, and some who do not understand or some unbelievers come in, will they not say that you are out of your mind? But if an unbeliever or someone who does not understand comes in while everybody is prophesying, he will be convinced by all that he is a sinner and will be judged by all, and the secrets of his heart will be laid bare. So he will fall down and worship God, exclaiming, "God is really among you!"

When the scripture says "everyone was prophesying," it literally means that everyone participated. In those early house churches, everyone was involved. The word *prophesy* in this passage refers to each person ministering or speaking into the life of the unbeliever who entered the house.

When the unbeliever entered the room of Christ followers, prophesy began to flow naturally as the individual believers longed to minister to the needs of the unbelieving visitor. God's power was manifest in their midst, first moving in the midst of transformed believers and then overflowing to the lost among them.

And so it is today. Cell groups come to life when an unbeliever attends. The members exercise their gifts in a new, fresh way. Believers minister to unbelievers and unbelievers give believers a reason for ministry. Spiritual gifts come alive when this mix comes together. There's a new desire to serve and give to others. As the world beholds this type of practical love and unity in action, Christ tells us that they will be won to himself. They will not only hear the gospel, but they will see the gospel lived out. Ultimately more and better disciples will be made.

Chapter Six

DISCIPLESHIP THROUGH MULTIPLICATION

In February 2010, I had an "aha moment." I was speaking at a cell conference in Dallas, Texas with Mario Vega, lead pastor of the Elim Church in San Salvador. I sat down, and it was Mario's turn to speak. Mario's theme was the biblical basis for cell ministry and during his talk he said, "Multiplication is the result of the health of the cell." Mario explained that multiplication is not the goal. Rather, the goal is making disciples who make new disciples. As those disciples are formed and developed in a caring, loving environment, multiplication is the result. Knowing that Mario was the lead pastor of one of the fastest growing churches in the world, I listened intently to what he had to say about cell multiplication.

As I think back, I probably heard those words many times previously, but I wasn't ready to really hear them until that moment. It had become increasingly clear to me that multiplication could not be the primary goal—like I had previously thought in 1997. [60]

It would take many more years and living in a different context to understand that multiplication is not the goal. Rather it's the result of a focus on making disciples who make disciples. In other words, a healthy disciple is formed and shaped in a life-giving cell.

We should desire to make as many healthy disciples as possible, but it's equally important to understand that multiplying a cell group isn't the same thing as making a healthy disciple. It's possible to multiply a cell group and not even have a leader, as some cell churches have done. These churches have multiplied cell groups by asking one leader to facilitate more than one group. Yet having a lot of groups is not the purpose of cell ministry, and such activity can have harmful side effects, like burn-out and discouragement. The mission is to make disciples who make disciples—just like Jesus taught.

DON'T FORCE MULTIPLICATION

When I truly caught the vision that healthy cells multiply because disciples are prepared and ready to start new groups, I began to focus on making disciples and stopped worrying about how long it took to multiply the group. Until then, I was more concerned about multiplying the group within a certain time period or on a planned multiplication date—even if healthy disciples were not developed. It was a mechanical, knee-jerk reaction, and I was placing the cart before the horse.

I remember one cell group, for example, in which we enjoyed sweet fellowship and community. The main couple who attended the group had a lot of non-Christian friends, booming secular business in the city, and loved the group. Yet, after a certain amount of time, I felt we needed to multiply because that's what cells were supposed to do. The problem was that disciples were not prepared. This couple correctly realized that I was forcing a multiplication before the right time—something that I only later realized. They eventually left the church.

Yes, new births will be painful, and discomfort is part of the growing experience, but I also think we need to make sure that the pain isn't self-inflicted through man-motivated, forced activity. The emphasis should always be on making disciples who make disciples and the result is multiplication—not the other way around.

As I've grown in my understanding of healthy multiplication, I've also changed my cell definition to highlight making new disciples that results in multiplication:

> A group of three to fifteen people who meet weekly outside the church building for the purpose of evangelism, community, and spiritual growth *with the goal of making disciples who make disciples* which results in multiplication.

In the past, I prioritized multiplication and *implied* that making disciples was the result. Yet, I've often passed over that *implication* and failed to practice it. As I travel around the world, I see many pastors falling into the same trap. They push multiplication as an end in itself, rather than the result of something greater—making disciples who make disciples. Prepared disciples are molded in nourishing, life-giving cell groups—just like healthy babies are shaped in healthy wombs.

FORMATION IN THE WOMB

The formation of a baby and the subsequent new birth is a miraculous process. One of the most wonderful moments of my life was seeing Sarah Comiskey born in Quito, Ecuador on September 16, 1991. I couldn't believe that what the doctor placed in our arms was a living, breathing human being. Yet, Sarah's birth didn't happen overnight. She was formed in an atmosphere that prepared her to face the challenges of new life.

Throughout the first three months, a baby grows at an astonishing rate, turning from a tiny group of cells into a fetus. The baby draws nutrition from its mother, and by month seven, the baby reaches nine inches. The baby's internal organs are maturing and now has a fully formed face. Some babies have even been photographed sucking their thumbs in the womb during the second trimester. The baby continues to gain weight rapidly and by the end of the seventh month has eyebrows and eyelashes. The baby's brain develops rapidly during the last trimester

The nutritional environment of a mother's womb affects the baby's health, not only at birth and during early infancy, but for the rest of his or her life. This means that the future health of the baby will be affected when the mother gets either too little of the right nutrients or too much of the wrong ones.

Just as a developing baby needs the proper conditions within the uterus to thrive outside, healthy disciples grow as they are developed in healthy cells. What are the key signs that disciples have been formed within the cell and ready to give birth?

SIGN #1: IS COMMUNITY TAKING PLACE?

Jesus chose twelve diverse disciples and took three years to mold them together as a single unit. It took that long for them to learn to look past their differences and love one another. Jesus told them that their impact on the world depended on the love they showed toward one another.

Jesus molds and shapes cell groups in the same way today. If a new cell multiplies that hasn't experienced true community, there's a good chance it won't survive. Before multiplication happens, those in the cell should first experience what it means to be the family of God. If community is not happening in the mother cell, what will the new group have to offer? Those new disciples in the womb of the cell need a chance to depend on their brothers and sisters in times of difficulties and struggle. Future disciples need the opportunity to consistently share transparently, ask for prayer, contribute praise reports, and pray for others.

They should have learned to deal with conflict in the group. Without conflict, believers won't exercise their muscles to grow deeper in their Christian faith. Peter says, "Above all, love each other deeply, because love covers over a multitude of sins" (1 Peter 4:7-8). The word *deeply* in Greek literally means to *stretch out*. It denotes the tense muscle activity of an athlete. Loving others requires the stretching out and exercising muscles we didn't know existed. We have to cover the sins of our brothers and sisters with a love that only the Holy Spirit can provide. This type of love doesn't come naturally—only supernaturally. Pressing through the conflict to community is worth the pain, and it's not wise to rush the multiplication process until community is happening. Remember the goal isn't simply a new cell group. Rather, the goal is healthy disciples who are forged in God-given community.

SIGN #2: IS EVERYONE PARTICIPATING?

The New Testament house churches were flexible and dynamic. Everyone participated and Paul could say to the house church in Ephesus, ". . . the whole body, joined and held together by every supporting ligament, grows and builds itself up in love, as each part does its work" (Ephesians 4:16). Paul wrote to another house church in Colossae, "Let the word of Christ dwell in you richly as you teach and admonish one another with all wisdom, and as you sing psalms, hymns and spiritual songs with gratitude in your hearts to God" (Colossians 3:16). Paul wanted the house church believers to freely share, to encourage one another, and to rejoice in God's goodness. We don't see a rigid agenda or one person giving the Bible study. Rather, the meeting was a time to minister to one another and meet needs. The Holy Spirit used each member as an instrument of edification. The members enjoyed each other's presence, laughed together, and experienced rich fellowship. Robert Banks writes, "We find no suggestion that these meetings were conducted with the kind of solemnity and formality that surrounds most weekly Christian gatherings today." [61]

A group is not ready to multiply unless the group members are actively ministering to one another, applying the word of God to real life, and actively using their gifts. The disciples who will eventually lead the daughter cell are best prepared in this type of environment. Future disciples will also need to know how to identify their own gifts and help others in finding and using theirs. They need to first witness an organic, dynamic cell group, so they can reproduce the same thing in the daughter cell.

SIGN #3: IS THE GROUP EVANGELIZING?

If the mother cell group has not practiced evangelism together, most likely the daughter group won't practice it either. And if the mother cell is ingrown, future disciples who will lead the new group won't have a positive mental image of what they are supposed to do.

Some have taught that the mother cell needs to win a certain number of people to Jesus before multiplication occurs. I disagree. God has to give the fruit. Our part is to sow the seed. The responsibility of the cell group is to consistently reach out, both as a group and individually. Maybe the daughter cell will see far more fruit than the mother cell! But if the mother cell is not actively evangelizing, the new disciples who will guide the new leadership team won't know what to do. If the mother cell leader only populates the cell with people already in the larger gathering (celebration), the cell will reproduce after its own ingrown kind.

It's also true that disciples are formed as they exercise their muscles in developing relationships with non-Christians, serving in the community, praying for non-Christian friends, contributing ideas to cell outreach, and inviting people to the cell groups. If we believe the goal of the cell is to make disciples who make disciples, it's important that the potential disciples have been using their evangelistic muscles to reach out and win new people.

SIGN #4: ARE NEW DISCIPLES FORMED?

If no one is being formed in the group to lead the next group, multiplication won't take place. It's possible to envision and even set goals for cell multiplication, but if a potential new disciple-maker is not moving through the birth canal, multiplication won't take place.

Fully-functioning Cell Member

The first step is for cell leaders to observe the members in the cell, paying close attention to their character development. Those who will serve on a new leadership team must be FAST:

Faithful, Available, Servant-hearted, and Teachable. Have they demonstrated these characteristics within the cell? Do they attend consistently? Show up on time? Are they prepared to pray, lead worship, guide the ice-breaker, or facilitate the cell lesson?

The Bible is clear that a growing disciple needs to have a good testimony toward outsiders (1 Timothy 3:7). You don't want to lift someone up who will later malign the church. I think it's also essential that team members walk in a certain amount of holiness (Hebrews 12:14). I'm not referring to perfection, because that won't happen this side of heaven. I am referring to freedom from major sins, such as fornication, pornography, and so forth.

Secondly, has the person been tested to actually lead the cell meeting? A new disciple is not ready to lead the new group unless he has fully participated in the mother group—including leading the lesson on more than one occasion.

Completed Discipleship Equipping

We'll learn in chapter 8 that future disciples must complete the discipleship equipping, which teaches doctrine, spiritual disciplines, evangelism, and leadership development. Group members, for example, will learn within the group how to evangelize, but the discipleship equipping will teach them the specifics of how to share the gospel, prepare testimonies, and implement the biblical basis for evangelism. The discipleship equipping path is intimately linked with cell ministry and furthers the process of making disciples who make disciples that results in cell multiplication. Cell churches use different terms for this discipleship equipping such as training track or school of leaders.

The discipleship equipping takes the new believer from point A to point B. Everyone in the church should go through it. The equipping is specific, and the process produces disciples who make other disciples through new cell groups. Cell church equipping features clarity and "do-ability." There is a definite beginning and ending and a new person entering the church can readily understand what it takes to go from A to B.

So while the new disciples are being formed within the cell, they are also being shaped by the discipleship equipping that takes place outside the cell group. It's this one-two punch that helps cell churches excel in the discipleship-making process.

Character Check

Even though a person has completed the discipleship equipping, faithfully participated in the cell group, and is considered FAST (faithful, available, servant-hearted, and teachable), it doesn't mean that the new disciple is ready to lead a group—or even be part of a discipleship team. There might be hidden character flaws that would hinder leadership involvement and ultimately cause problems down the road. This is why it's important that upper level leadership approve the new candidate before he or she is placed on a new leadership team.

Love Alive Church, in Tegucigalpa, Honduras, is a great example of the benefit of requiring a character check for candidates for a new cell leadership team. Love Alive requires that the pastor interview each new potential team leader. A series of questions are asked about the person's devotional life, marriage, available time for the church, and personal attitudes. When I first observed this process, I thought it was overly restrictive and too time-consuming, but over the years I've seen the importance of this quality control. It helps ensure (not guarantee) that the leader will remain strong under pressure and that the cell group has a better chance of surviving. And I was told that only one out of ten cell groups fail at Love Alive Church.

SIGN #5: IS A LEADERSHIP TEAM IN PLACE?

I'm more and more convinced that a cell shouldn't multiply until a team of disciples is in place and ready to lead the new group. This means those who start a new cell have fully participated in the mother cell and have gone through the equipping process.

The Biblical Norm

A plurality of leaders guided the early house church. Paul, for example, told the leaders of the Ephesian church that the Holy Spirit had made them "overseers" of the flock (Acts 20:28). When writing to the church at Philippi, Paul greeted the congregation and, separately, the "overseers" (Philippians 1:1). When he wrote to Titus, Paul directed the appointment of elders, whom he also identified with the functions of "overseer" (Titus 1:5-7). Whether they are designated as a "body of elders" (1 Timothy 4:14) or simply as "elders," this form of leadership was always exercised by a group of people rather than by one single individual (Acts 20:17; 1 Timothy 5:17; Titus 1:5; James 5:14; 1 Peter 5:1-4). Michael Green says about early church leadership,

> Leadership was always plural: the word "presbyter" from which we derive "priest" is regularly used in the plural when describing Christian ministry in the New Testament. They were a leadership team, supporting and encouraging

one another, and doubtless making up for each other's deficiencies. This team leadership is very evident in the missionary journeys of the New Testament, and Acts 13 is particularly interesting. It indicates not only a plural leadership in Antioch, consisting of five members, but diverse types of leadership: some were "prophets" relying on charismatic gifts, while others were "teachers" relying on study of the Scriptures. [62]

Even the first apostles operated as a team. While guiding the Jerusalem church, they shared the leadership of the congregation with a group of elders (Acts 15:4, 6, 22), who remained long after the apostles were gone (Acts 21:18). The New Testament writers avoid the idea of one, single leader. The norm for the early churches was to have a team of pastors rather than only one. In addition to elders, two churches are mentioned as having deacons (Philippians 1:1; 1 Timothy 3:8, 12). Whatever their functions may have been, their services were also provided on the basis of shared leadership since they are always mentioned in the plural.

I find it much more liberating to tell future disciple-makers that they will not be leading the group individually but will function in a team. Potential disciple-makers feel more secure when knowing they won't have to do everything themselves. New groups are also much healthier when led by a leadership team. But how do we make this practical?

One Person in Charge

Even with the emphasis of plurality of New Testament leadership, there are indications in the New Testament that a point person led the house church teams (e.g., 1 Timothy 5:17). I have coached churches who didn't have a point person due to their Scriptural convictions about equality of team ministry. While I liked their team spirit, I discovered that when no one is in charge, it's common for no one to take responsibility, which leads to lack of clarity and direction.

I believe it's best to have one person guide the discipleship team, although it's essential that the point person lead the team with a servant attitude. Scripture is clear that those in charge need to lead in humility, rather than a controlling, dominating spirit. Jesus said the greatest in leadership would be the servant of all (Matthew 20:25-28; John 13:13-17).

Extend the Team

Too often in small group ministry, we've emphasized one or two people who we call *leaders*. But why limit the team to two people? Why not have a team of three, like Jesus, or four or five, like the apostle Paul? Not only can small group responsibilities be distributed more widely on a larger team, but there's more possibility of multiplication.

It seems to me that when we use the term *co-leader* or *assistant leader,* we are cutting ourselves off to additional team members. Why not just use the term *team leader* or *team member* and slowly add new potential disciple-makers to the team.

With more on the discipleship team, more people will actually attend faithfully each week (assuming that the team members are always there), and more people can help with the functions within the group (e.g., bringing refreshments, worship, prayer, lesson, evangelistic outreach, and so forth).

Focus on the Giftedness of Each Team Member

Team leadership functions should be distributed according to the giftedness of each member. If Joe has the gift of evangelism, he should be responsible to lead the small group outreach. If Nancy has the gift of mercy, she can help in the visitation of a hospitalized member or organize the visitation. If Jose has the gift of teaching, he can rotate in leading the small group lesson or in the taking a member through the church approved discipleship equipping. If Jeanie has the gift of apostleship, she should be spearheading the next multiplication. If Andrew has the gift of administration, he can be in charge of distributing small group responsibilities—who brings refreshments, leads worship, prayer, lesson, and so forth.

Communication as a Team

Once you've established who will be on the team, it's essential to emphasize love and servanthood. It's important to establish the rule that team members will talk directly to other team members, rather than gossiping, especially to avoid the subtle trap of gossiping in the name of praying for so-and-so. Absolute honesty and willingness to walk through conflict—and actually growing through it—are important traits that make or break effective team ministry. Remember that even the great apostle Paul experienced issues with his team (Acts 15:1-4) and with team member Barnabas (Acts 15:36-41). Paul's willingness to walk through these conflicts honestly and face these issues directly resulted in continuation of his great ministry. Team ministry can be intense, and therefore it's essential to keep short accounts, allow love to cover a multitude of sins, and especially to develop friendship among team members. In fact, friendship is the glue that sustains the team over time.

How can you do this? I recommend touching base by phone, texting, email, talking to each other at church, and personally meeting one another. How often? The more the better, but I would say at least once per month the team should meet together for fellowship and planning.

What should you cover in the group meeting? First, it's a time to pray for one another and the small group. Second, get to know each member of the small group. What are their needs? Does John need a personal one-on-one meeting? Does Jane need more responsibility in the group? Who in the cell group needs to be encouraged to go through the church-wide discipleship equipping? Third, assign responsibilities for the small group meeting.

MULTIPLYING DISCIPLES

As mentioned in the introduction, Mario Vega believes that healthy cells multiply. Before Mario became lead pastor of Elim Church San Salvador, many leaders would start and lead more than one cell during the year to fulfill the church's goal (often under pressure). When Mario Vega assumed leadership of Elim San Salvador, he starting promoting a healthier view of multiplication, one based on making disciples rather than just starting new groups. In fact, he stopped counting groups that didn't have their own leader because he felt such groups were padding the Elim statistics, but not fulfilling the goal of making disciples who make disciples.

Rather than making new groups, we need to emphasize making disciples. Abe Huber is the founder and pastor of a Brazilian cell church movement that has grown to almost ten thousand cell groups. He writes:

From my experience, the key to great cells is great discipleship.

The big question is: "How can we guarantee that all will be cared for and truly discipled?" To begin a process of discipleship in your church, you have to take the lead and be an example. First of all, you as the pastor need to have a mentor/discipler with whom you are accountable for your spiritual life. I'm referring to someone who will pray with you and give you counsel. This person should be someone who you look up to, who is also respected by your congregation, and who gives you spiritual covering.

Once you have a discipler, it is always a lot easier to encourage the whole church to want to be discipled. You should then start discipling some of your key men, one-on-one. Spend quality time with them, helping them with their relationship with the Lord, and in their relationship with their family.

It is also very important that your key disciples become leaders and supervisors of your cells. Your discipleship time with them will include mentoring them on how to effectively lead, multiply, and supervise their cells.

You and your disciples have to remember this: Our priority is not to multiply the cells. Rather, cell multiplication is the natural outgrowth of effective disciple-making. Our priority is to make "disciple-making disciples." As leaders we should be reproducing new leaders. If your disciples are cell leaders, and if they are being effective in their discipleship, they will definitely be reproducing new cell leaders!

Lovingly, I have to remind you, however, that you can only reproduce in others what has first been produced in you. You can only give birth to new leaders, if you humbly permit someone to speak into your life and allow the "birth pangs" of Christ to be formed in you. You will only be a good discipler, if you first become a good disciple. That is why it is so crucial that you model discipleship. Your key leaders and members of the church will also want to be discipled and mentored as they see how much you value your discipler and receive from him.

I believe that this is just the beginning of a discipleship revolution that will transform you and your ministries! [63]

The focus of making disciples through cell ministry remains true across cultures and boundaries. In some places, like Spain, multiplying new disciples might take a long, long time. In other places, like Brazil, the multiplication of groups and disciples can happen rapidly because of the receptivity. While multiplication frequency differs, the process is the same.

ENVISIONING NEW GROUPS

Should each leader set a goal for a new cell group? In my earlier days of cell research and ministry, I would have said, "Yes, all cells need to set multiplication goals." It didn't matter if the cell had any idea whether it could multiply, but I felt it was best for the cell to set a goal for multiplication. Part of the reason was my original research that showed that cell groups that actually had goals for multiplication multiplied faster than those who did not have one.

But does this fact mean that the cell leader from the first day of the cell should say, "We're going to multiply on such and such a date." Talking about multiplication before the cell has formed a sense of community can do more harm than good. First, it can hinder community. The people immediately feel they will be saying good-bye very soon and won't take the time to establish close relationships. Some might not even commit to the group for fear of a quick departure. Second, it places fear in some people that they will be "leaders" before they have had a natural chance to develop in the cell and work through the discipleship equipping component of the discipleship process.

I think it's much better for the team leadership to work behind the scenes. As leaders grow through participating, they will grasp the purpose of stepping out and being part of a discipleship team. We also know that discipleship equipping is a crucial component in the discipleship process, so it's best for the team leader to invite all members to take the discipleship equipping—rather than immediately telling they will be part of a future multiplication team! In other words, they'll understand team leadership better when they are going through the discipleship equipping and have had more time to participate in the cell.

I asked one cell church pastor how he had become so successful in cell multiplication. He said to me, "My people are born again in the cell and learn to speak the language of cell multiplication. Like a baby learning a new language, they understand that they are called to be disciples and form new cell groups. They know their purpose is to reach out and infiltrate new neighborhoods for Jesus." When a church reaches the point of seeing new spiritual births in the cell group and then maturing these new people through the natural process of cell discipleship, the cell becomes a powerful tool in the hand of God to reach out to a hurt and dying world.

Part 3

HOW THE CELL SYSTEM MAKES DISCIPLES

Chapter Seven

DISCIPLESHIP IN THE LARGER GATHERING

Many don't like the word _cell_. They equate it with a prison cell or small secret communistic gathering, which are also called _cells_. And because of these negative connotations, I welcome churches to change the word to something more palatable, like life groups (although I tell churches to avoid changing the cell definition).[2] With so many negative connotations, why do many still use the word _cell_?

2 I go into more detail about groups name in this article: http://www.joelcomiskeygroup. com/articles/basics/NAMEcell.html. While it's okay to change the name, I highly recommend maintaining a quality definition like: groups of three to fifteen that meet weekly outside the church building for the purpose of evangelism, community, and spiritual growth with the goal of making disciples who make disciples which results in multiplication.

One of the main reasons is because of the comparison with the human body. A special symbiotic relationship exists between individual cells and the human body as a whole. One can't exist without the other. Biological cells are not independent entities that function on their own. They depend on the ecosystem of the rest of the body, and the health of the entire body draws from each individual cell.

A human body is composed of around one hundred trillion individual cells that work together to produce a fully functioning human body. Sometimes when just a single cell becomes altered, it can dramatically change the whole body. This occurs in the development of cancer. From the perspective of the altered cell(s), it may seem like it is doing no wrong. It is living better, longer, and may be more fruitful. But this is a disaster from the level of the human body. The cells' characteristics have now changed and will inevitably affect their interrelationship with the rest of the body. The good news is that cancer cells are normally destroyed before they take over. How? The human body sends out white blood cells that actively scan the body for abnormal cells, destroying them before they can develop into actual cancer.

Cell churches function a lot like human bodies. Individual cells are not allowed to act like independent entities that have no connection beyond themselves. Rather, each cell is part of a greater whole and receives nourishment from other parts of the body. Each cell works together with the other cells to fulfill a common purpose. Gathering those cells together in larger gatherings enhances that common purpose by ensuring cell health, reminding cells of the common vision, and providing teaching that each of the cells would not otherwise receive. The ultimate goal of the larger gathering of the cells is for each member to become more like Jesus.

THE CONNECTION BETWEEN CELL AND THE LARGER GATHERING

The connection between cell and celebration (larger gathering) is biblical. Scripture teaches a clear relationship between the New Testament house churches. The house churches that Paul planted, in other words, were part of a larger unit. Gehring writes, "Many NT scholars believe that both forms—small house churches and the whole church as a unit at that location—existed side by side in early Christianity." [64]

Paul's own leadership was crucial in linking house churches together. We see Paul and Silas in Acts 16:4 traveling from town to town, delivering the decisions reached by the apostles and elders in Jerusalem. Most of the time, those house churches networked together with other house churches but only met occasionally for larger group gatherings.

However, in at least two cases, the Jerusalem church and the Corinthian church, the cells connected in a larger gathering on a consistent, ongoing basis. In Jerusalem, the early church met in houses to participate in the Lord's supper and fellowship, but then those same house churches gathered together in the temple to hear the apostles teaching. Acts 2:46-47 says, "Every day they continued to meet together in the temple courts. They broke bread in their homes and ate together with glad and sincere hearts, praising God and enjoying the favor of all the people. And the Lord added to their number daily those who were being saved." We see here both the house church meetings as well as those house churches coming together to hear the apostles teaching.

The second example is in Corinth. Paul says, "So if the whole church comes together and everyone speaks in tongues, and some who do not understand or some unbelievers come in, will they not say that you are out of your mind?" (1 Corinthians 14:23). Paul speaking about the whole church coming together implies that at other times the Christians in Corinth met separately in smaller house churches.

Whether meeting together in a larger gathering regularly or occasionally, the house churches in the New Testament were connected, and this connection has important implications for discipleship. Disciples were developed in both the house church and the gathered assembly of believers. But how does this discipleship take place in the larger gathering?

HIGHER LEVEL TEACHING

Discipleship in the cell is practical. The purpose is to apply God's word to each member. The goal is for each person to go away transformed rather than simply informed. This requires the cell leader to facilitate the discussion and allow individual members the chance to share, work out their problems, and exercise their gifts to minister to others. I encourage cell leaders not to play *Bible answer man*. Rather more in-depth teaching happens in the larger celebration.

One of the key ways discipleship takes place in the larger gathering is via the teaching of God's inerrant word. Paul's exhortation to Timothy applies today, "Preach the word; be prepared in season and out of season; correct, rebuke and encourage—with great patience and careful instruction. For the time will come when men will not put up with sound doctrine. Instead, to suit their own desires, they will gather around them a great number of teachers to say what their itching ears want to hear" (2 Timothy 4:2-3).

In the early church, we read that the early believers devoted themselves to the apostles' teaching (Acts 2:42). The apostles had a better handle on Christ's teaching because they had been with him for three years. They were able to help the house church members grow in their faith. In the same way, those who have received additional training in God's word are able to teach the rest of the church and assist in the discipleship process. The pastor or staff can tackle the difficult, hard to understand passages of scripture and fill in the doctrinal gaps. Pastors can also apply God's word to the particular needs within the congregation. For example, it's one thing to listen to a general sermon on the radio, but when a pastor preaches God's word to a specific congregation, the application is much richer since the pastor knows the flock and can direct God's word to the needs of the congregation.

Perhaps, cell leaders and members have brought questions to the supervisors and staff. The pastor might prioritize those topics within the preaching. I've noticed in cell churches around the world that often those with the gift of teaching are first identified in the cell. As these people become cell leaders and supervisors, they are sometimes asked to become part of the pastoral team. They understand the cell system because they were born again into it. When they preach God's word, they are able to use illustrations and real-life experiences to fine-tune cell members and leaders.

Most cell groups use the passage or theme of the pastor's message to guide the cell lesson. In this way, the cell members can ask questions, gain clarification, and especially apply the spiritual truths that were taught in the sermon. I have become increasingly convinced of the effectiveness of basing the cell lesson on the sermon theme that is taught in the larger gathering.

CELEBRATING TOGETHER

Worship in the cell group can be an intimate experience. Every believer can ask for prayer, offer areas of thanksgiving, read scripture, share needs, and apply God's word to their daily lives. I've noticed, however, that cell groups often have more difficulties entering into worship in the small group context. The reasons might include the lack of musical talent, lack of someone who can play an instrument, embarrassment to sing out, and feelings of vocal inadequacy.

Worship in the larger group can help those in the small group. Transformation takes place in the larger worship service as the cell members are directed by an anointed worship leader to enter God's presence and receive empowering as a result.

There is something powerful about a larger group gathering that inspires people to seek after the living God. In the Old Testament we read how the Lord instituted annual festivals and large gatherings for his people. This gave them a sense of the bigger picture of what God was doing in the world, and a chance to be inspired by the awesome majesty of God. Something similar takes place in the larger worship gathering. There's a wonderful symbiotic relationship between cells and the rest of the body as the larger group gathers to reflect on God's majestic greatness.

Worship in the larger gathering is a time to practice Christ's words, "Come to me, all you who are weary and burdened, and I will give you rest. Take my yoke upon you and learn from me, for I am gentle and humble in heart, and you will find rest for your souls. For my yoke is easy and my burden is light" (Matthew 11:28-29). Those ministering in cells will function better as they are refreshed. Life beats people down and there's nothing like worship to lift up God's people and remind them that God is in control.

I appreciated hearing one worship leader tell the congregation to soak in the presence of God and allow God to minister directly to their hearts. He encouraged them to close their eyes and just listen to God's voice. He told them not to worry about posture or singing ability but just to receive God's love and grace. Rather than insisting that the congregation sing louder or yelling out, "I can't hear you," this anointed worship leader told the church to rest in God's presence and receive his refreshment. The best worship experiences promote this type of transformational attitude.

In many cell churches the worship leader first used his or her gifts and talents in the cell group and then was asked to lead on a larger scale. This is helpful because the worship leader knows the needs of those in the congregation and understands that cell members, leaders, supervisors, and staff need God's refreshing in order to keep on giving out.

Cell and celebration work together in the discipleship process. Cell discipleship is more intensive and hands-on. Celebration discipleship helps members to see the larger picture as everyone worships in a festive environment. Both are essential in the process of becoming more like Jesus.

EXTENDED FAMILY GATHERINGS

Discipleship takes place in cell groups as each person is able to share deep needs and experience the family of God in an intimate way. Separating from those close relationships when multiplication happens can be a painful process that is often resisted by the group members for fear of losing relationships with others in the group. In fact, the word *division* is often associated with cell multiplication. Many feel that multiplication disrupts relationships, and they want to avoid it at all costs.

Although painful, multiplication does not mean separation, especially when the cell groups are regularly meeting together in the larger gathering. The larger gathering provides a way for the family of God to once again connect on a larger level.

Close friends that were at one time in the same cell group can see each other, relive old times, and receive renewed refreshment before or after the service. They might even sit by each other during the worship service.

I view the family in the larger gathering as a time for the extended family of God to gather, refresh one another and grow closer to Jesus in the process.

Many traditional churches are what I call *single cell* churches because they want to do everything together. If there is a birthday, they all have to celebrate it together. If there is an activity, all have to be present. Such churches will never grow beyond the closed circle of friendships, and the single cell mentality leads to stagnation and exclusivity.

In the cell church, however, the intimate friendships are developed in the cell. The larger gathering promotes the renewal of a diversity of extended family relationships. Kirk is a good friend of mine. We were in the same cell group years ago. He now leads a family cell and I'm part of a men's group. Yet, Kirk and I enjoy each other's company and encourage each other during the Sunday gatherings. We ask about each other's family, share prayer requests, and generally encourage each other in the Christian life.

VISION CASTING

Cells members receive vision and direction from their leader to use their gifts, evangelize as a group, practice the one anothers of scripture, and even receive discipleship equipping (next chapter). Cell groups provide a wonderful context for members to fulfill God's vision for their lives and to move ahead in ministry. Yet cell groups are part of a greater whole, just like biological cells. Biological cells are not supposed to chart their own course. Rather, they have a specific part to play within the larger body.

During the larger gatherings, the lead pastor of a cell church has the opportunity to disciple those in the cell and those leading cells by casting vision, direction, and offering encouragement. Cell leaders can easily be discouraged because of problems in the group, lack of fruit, or personal time commitments. Wise cell church pastors use the preaching, the announcements, testimonies and other means to remind leaders of their eternal rewards, the great things God is doing, and the need for persistence.

The new cell members soon realize that they are part of a larger group of people who are speaking the same language and have the same objective to win the world for Jesus. Soon the congregation begins to realize that cell life is the normal Christian life and that attending the celebration service is only one part of that reality. Church goers who are not yet attending a cell group are encouraged to be involved in a cell to capture the full benefits of what the church really is.

Most churches make time for announcements and testimonies. Some churches attach them to the end of the service or before the preaching. Does it make a difference which announcements receive priority? I believe so. In the cell church, cell ministry is central to all that takes place. Why not make it a priority in the announcements? These are some ideas:

- Asking a cell member who has been transformed through relational ministry—new friendships, special ministry times—to share what God has done.
- Hearing the testimony of someone who has received healing within the cell group.
- Presenting a new multiplication leader to the entire church.

Both the person giving the testimony and those hearing will grow in their relationship with Jesus as a result. Those attending the Sunday celebration need to realize that the primary pastoral services of the church are offered through the cell system. If they need ministry and help, they can find it in a loving cell group.

Vision casting for cell ministry can find a great friend in the bulletin or other advertisements in the church. Some churches don't have a bulletin, but if there's even an occasional handout, it's a great time to give cell ministry its proper place. I suggest that the bulletin in the cell church highlight a cell testimony of how people's lives have been transformed through cell ministry.

I'm coaching one church that has twelve cells and one hundred twenty-five people gathered on Sunday. The bulletin, a two-sided sheet of paper, lists all the cell groups each week on the front page. The statement is made each Sunday: "We're making disciples through cell ministry."

A visitor to the church should be able to detect the philosophy and priority of the church from the Sunday morning service. I encourage cell-based churches to have a cell information table where they lay out relevant books on cell ministry, the weekly cell lesson, a box to place cell reports, and other pertinent information about cell ministry.

It's a great idea to post in the foyer a map of the city with each cell group pinned on it. This map explains where the cells are located, their focus (e.g., family cells, women's cells, youth cells, and so forth), and when they meet. A volunteer worker or secretary should be available to answer questions each week and connect new people to cell ministry.

It's not easy to adapt to the cell model. People are accustomed to their old ways and habits. They must be reminded of the cell church focus by what they see in church during the worship service.

REACHING THE HARVEST

Individual cell groups are great to strengthen the muscles of each member through net fishing, but throwing out a much larger net is also very effective. Many cell churches promote evangelistic events in the larger gathering during the year. The cell groups are intimately involved in these large group events.

I've seen many videos of the evangelistic events at the Elim Church in San Salvador that have attracted more than one hundred fifty thousand people. The reason for the success was that each cell member actively participated in inviting, administrating, and praying for the event. Each cell member, cell group, sector, zone, and district worked together in harmony to reach people for Jesus. Rather than primarily being a massive rally of seekers, the event was carefully administrated by color coded sectors, zones, and districts so everyone knew where to sit, what bus to use, and how to follow-up.

Granted, the massive rallies, like the ones Elim initiates are rare. But cell churches mobilize the cell troops on a smaller scale as well. I've seen various cell churches use "Friend's Day" with great effectiveness. The church mobilizes the cell groups to invite their close associates to a special seeker service on a particular day. The transformation takes place not only in the lives of those who receive Jesus but in each member, cell, and leader as all work together as a disciplined army to achieve a greater objective. A different set of muscles is required for the larger event. It requires availability, willingness to work as a team and follow orders, submission, faithfulness, and commitment. Future disciples are nurtured in the atmosphere of missions.

TWO-WINGED CHURCH

Bill Beckham coined the term *two-winged church* to describe the emphasis of both the small and large group in the cell church. Both wings help the bird fly. Beckham often uses the following parable to describe the cell church:

> A church with two wings was once created; it could fly high into the presence of God. One day the serpent, who had no wings, challenged the church to fly with one wing only, that is the large gathering wing. With much effort the church managed to fly, and the serpent strongly applauded it. With this experience, the church became convinced that it could fly very well with only one wing. God, the creator of the church, was very sad. The church with only one wing could barely rise above the ground, and it just flew in circles without being able to move from its point of origin. The church settled down and started to gain weight and became lazy, beaming with a purely earthly life. Finally, the creator formed a new church with its two wings. Once again God had a church that could fly into His presence and sing His joyful praises. [65]

A church with two wings is better equipped to make disciples who make disciples than a church that emphasizes one or the other exclusively. Both are important in the process of discipleship.

Chapter Eight
DISCIPLESHIP
EQUIPPING

As I've watched World War II documentaries or read books on World War II, one constant thread is that the soldier's boot camp experience was invaluable. Over and over the surviving soldiers talked about how much they hated, yet needed, the boot camp training. In actual battle, they would respond subconsciously to what they learned through the repeated boot camp drills. The monotonous workouts they loathed during boot camp saved their lives by helping them to respond efficiently and automatically in the battle.

All believers are on the front lines of spiritual warfare, whether they like it or not. Satan and his demons want to destroy the Church of Jesus Christ. To defeat the enemy and live victoriously, the Church needs to draw on biblical truth that comes from deep discipleship equipping. I'm referring to the essentials of the Christian life: how to pray and read the Bible, submitting to the Lordship of Christ, recognizing spiritual darkness, having a daily quiet time, and how to share the gospel message. Effective cell churches proactively develop all members through discipleship equipping that prepares them for the battle, just like boot camp.

Churches that produce disciple-makers know that tomorrow's spiritual leaders are today's spiritual children, spiritual adolescents, and spiritual teenagers. Many churches, on the other hand, have failed to equip members for future ministry. After all, there are so many present pressures. It seems absurd to think beyond the now. It's even possible for a church to initiate a cell ministry and to immediately produce many new groups. Further probing, however, often reveals that the initial growth was simply a changing of the guard. Established leaders that at one time maintained the cherished programs were relocated to lead cell groups. But without an established system for discipling current cell group members that will become new disciple-makers, cell ministry comes to a screeching halt.

Strong cell group churches, in contrast, develop discipleship equipping systems that carry the new Christian from conversion to forming part of a cell team. Because the top leadership realizes that equipping new disciple-makers is their chief task, they prioritize establishing a strong discipleship equipping system.

KEY DISTINCTIONS BETWEEN THE LESSON AND EQUIPPING

People are often confused about the difference between the discipleship equipping and the cell lesson. That is, they assume the discipleship equipping is the same thing as the cell lesson and that the cell facilitator teaches the discipleship equipping during the cell group. However, the lesson and the equipping are two distinct entities:

- The cell lesson: This is what the cell facilitator uses during the cell meeting. The lesson is normally based on the pastor's weekly sermon and is comprised of questions that focus on application that leads to transformation.
- The discipleship equipping: This is a series of manuals that teach basic doctrine, evangelism, spiritual disciplines, and small group dynamics. It is taught *separately* from the cell meeting and normally takes six months to one year to complete.

The purpose of the cell lesson is to apply God's word to daily living and to evangelize non-Christians. It doesn't specifically explain how to pray, read the Bible, have a devotional time, receive freedom from besetting sin, and other aspects of the Christian life, which are essential for discipleship.

Knowing the need for specific teaching, cell churches have developed discipleship equipping called by a variety of names, such as training track, school of leaders, or equipping track. I like the phrase *discipleship equipping* because it connects the main goal of discipleship with the need for essential equipping.

Discipleship equipping should not be complicated but simple and doable. The average time frame to complete it is about nine months. Many cell churches have advanced discipleship equipping for those who complete the first level.

The discipleship equipping can take place in a variety of places. Many churches use their Sunday school hour for the equipping. Others like to do the equipping before the cell starts or after it's done. Others ask cell members to complete the discipleship equipping on their own and then ask those who have already gone through the equipping to mentor the new ones.

Many larger cell churches expect the staff to teach the discipleship equipping. Other cell churches request those who have completed the discipleship equipping to mentor those who are just starting it. Normally when a church begins the cell journey, the lead pastor teaches the discipleship equipping to those who comprise the first pilot group. Those who have completed the equipping can then help out in the equipping process.

CLEAR EQUIPPING FOCUS

The best discipleship equipping path features a clear-cut beginning and ending. In other words, there is a place to start and a place to finish. It is not like many traditional educational programs that simply teach people information with the hope that they will do something with the knowledge later. Paul Benjamin, criticizing the North American Sunday School, writes, ". . . this is a school from which no one ever graduates."[66]

"Helter-skelter" equipping takes place when the church establishes one general educational program. While the intentions are excellent, far too many people fall through the cracks. There is no easy way to track the progress of those passing through this type of system. As a result of the fuzziness, a large number of candidates drop out. Getting lost in the educational machinery is a recurring flaw in the "general education" approach.

Education is a lifetime process. Equipping, on the other hand, touches specific skills and lasts a limited time. Education never ends. It's helpful to first examine the difference between equipping and education. Neil F. McBride, Ed.D., Ph.D., makes a helpful clarification:

Education is an expanding activity; starting with where a person is at, it provides concepts and information for developing broader perspectives and the foundations for making future analysis and decisions. On the other hand, training is a narrowing activity; given whatever a person's present abilities are, it attempts to provide specific skills and the necessary understanding to apply those skills. The focus is on accomplishing a specific task or job. [67]

McBride's insight about equipping being a *narrowing activity* versus the *lifetime process* of education touches the nerve of cell church equipping. Understanding the specific purpose of discipleship equipping helps to focus on equipping potential disciple-makers who can form new cell teams, while not ignoring the general on-the-job education that all believers need over the long haul.

When a church concludes that every member is a potential disciple-maker who can form part of a new cell team, the logical step is to equip each person for that task. Ralph Neighbour writes, "Cell churches must take seriously the need to equip every incoming cell member. Cell members will stagnate who are simply invited to attend cells, without clear equipping for service." [68]

The discipleship equipping is part of the overall cell ministry. It is not a "separate department" with a different administration. The discipleship equipping and the cell ministry "fit like a glove." They are one. In many cell churches the discipleship equipping begins in the cell (mentor-mentoree) because everyone in the church participates in a cell group. In other cell churches, although all new converts are immediately connected with a cell, most of the cell equipping takes place in larger groups within the church under the cell networks (i.e., clusters of cells gathered in geographical or homogeneous groupings).

MAKE IT DOABLE

One of the most important factors is whether or not the discipleship equipping is doable. Feasibility must guide the equipping. Will the person graduate from the equipping? Are the requirements too rigid? Are the options too few? Is there only one night available for the equipping? If so, only few will finish it.

I remember the early condition of the educational program in the El Batán Church, where I first ministered in Ecuador. On one occasion the pastoral team spent the whole day charting the educational process for all members in the church. It was a long, mind-numbing experience. Everything appeared immaculate on paper. We had solved our problems, theoretically. Our proud system failed because it wasn't doable or "trackable." We let it die, all by itself.

Through experiences like the one I just described, I've learned that feasibility is at the center of discipleship equipping. The successful cell churches include:

- Clear place to start
- Clear knowledge about where to go
- Clear idea of accomplishment

The bottom line is clarity. Successful cell churches aim for clarity, and maintain practicality. There is also clarity in tracking the progress of those in the equipping.

KEY PRINCIPLES

Most churches pass through multiple revisions of their equipping before finding the right fit. Initial failure often happens because a church tries to copy another church's equipping model in its entirety. Most often the church realizes eventually that the equipping model doesn't fit its context and unique identity.

To help you avoid this landmine, I've extracted six principles from some of the best cell church equipping models. These principles should undergird your equipping system, although the form of your equipping will be distinct. Here is a summary of the key principles

Principle #1: Keep the Equipping Track Simple

The best discipleship equipping is clear and simple. Most cell churches cover the following areas in their equipping:

- Basic doctrine
- Freedom from bondage
- Spiritual Disciplines
- Personal evangelism
- Multiplication

Principle #2: Provide Action Steps with the Equipping

People learn best when they apply what they learn. Make sure that your equipping is practical, and that you have an action step for each part of your equipping.

- *First step:* Basic Doctrine; action step of baptism in water
- *Second step:* Freedom from Bondage; action step of confession of sin
- *Third Step:* Spiritual Disciplines; action step of having a regular devotional time

- *Fourth Step:* Evangelism; action step of relational evangelism and inviting a non-Christian to the group
- *Fifth Step:* Cell Dynamics and Multiplication; action step of forming part of a cell team

Principle #3: Prepare a Second Level of Equipping for Small Group Leaders

Most cell churches continue to train those who have graduated from the first level and are part of a new discipleship team. To do this, they divide their equipping into at least two levels. The first level is the more basic level, which includes the five basic areas or steps mentioned above (each area is normally embodied in a manual).

The second level should include additional doctrinal courses, a spiritual warfare course, teaching on spiritual gifts, and so forth. There is a lot of room for creativity, and many excellent courses and materials are available. One cell church decided to use their denomination's theological education by extension equipping for this second level.

Those who have formed part of a cell team deserve special treatment because of their important, foundational role in the church. Offer them all the help and equipping that they need in order to be effective.

Some cell churches even offer a third and fourth level of equipping, all the way to pastoral ministry. Faith Community Baptist Church in Singapore features an extensive equipping program to prepare higher-level leaders. Bethany World Prayer Center hosts a three-year Bible school on its property. Neither church requires higher education for all cell leadership—it's simply provided for those who feel called to full-time ministry.

Principle #4: Use Only One Equipping Path

I counsel churches to have only one discipleship equipping path—although that one path can be adapted to age specific groups. After deciding on a church-wide discipleship equipping path (ideally both first and second levels), a church should ask everyone to pass through the same equipping. [69]

Principle #5: There Is No One Methodology for Implementing Your Equipping

Some people believe that the only way to equip new believers is one-on-one. Others disagree and prepare new believers in a group setting. Don't confuse the equipping methodology (where or how you equip people) with the material.

I've noticed a great variety of methodologies for implementing the equipping, such as one-on-one, one-on-two or -three, equipping after the cell group meeting, during Sunday school hour, seminars, retreats, or a combination of all of them. I suggest teaching the equipping path during the Sunday school hour, which is often connected to the worship service. Then I propose that those who can't attend during that time slot be given the freedom to take the same equipping before the cell starts, after the cell finishes, during a day-long equipping in a home, and any additional options to complete the equipping.

Principle #6: Continually Adjust and Improve the Equipping

You should be fine-tuning your equipping system continually. One cell church I studied had been working on their equipping for seven years; another had been in a process of development for ten, as they had been creating and recreating the tools. You will also need to adapt, adjust, and improve your equipping as you receive feedback from your members.

EQUIPPING THEMES

Cell church equipping is unique and creative. Often a church will use someone else's equipping material at first and then will develop their own.

The first area or step is basic Bible doctrine. All evangelical Christians would agree that the teaching of God's word is the foundation of the new believer's life. Does this mean that the new believer must take systematic theology 1, 2, 3, and 4 that takes four years to complete? Definitely not. I studied systematic theology in Bible college and seminary, but as a new believer I needed the milk of God's word—the basic principles.

One seminar attendee asked me, "What kind of Bible doctrine should I cover in my equipping series?" I told him that it was important to include basic teaching about God, sin, the person of Jesus Christ, salvation, the Holy Spirit, and the Church. I also told him that he must decide if this initial course would include six, nine, or fourteen lessons. The number of lessons in the first manual will depend on how much biblical doctrine your church deems necessary for the new believer.

The second area is freedom from bondage. So many believers are enslaved to bondages such as: unforgiveness, addictions, the occult, and other types of wicked behavior. Before the person comes to Christ, he or she probably picked up evil habits that continue to hinder after conversion. An encounter retreat, using carefully designed material, can help speed up the sanctification process by dealing with sinful weights that impede growth and fruitfulness.

The third area, inner-life development, focuses on spiritual disciplines but especially on having a quiet time. The goal is to help new believers feed themselves. This step is summed up in the saying, "Give a person a fish and you feed him for a day; teach him how to fish and you feed him for a lifetime."

The fourth area, evangelism, teaches the person how to share his or her faith, not only individually but in a group setting. Each believer needs to learn how to lead someone else to Jesus Christ. This stage explains the plan of salvation in a systematic, step-by-step process. Beyond learning the content of the gospel presentation, the believer must also learn how to develop friendships with non-Christians. The effectiveness of small group evangelism is also highlighted, and equipping is given on how the cell functions like a team to evangelize non-Christians as well as providing the ideal atmosphere for non-believers.

The final area covers how to facilitate a cell group and be part of a new cell team. The manual for this stage should cover the basics of cell ministry, small group dynamics (e.g., how to listen well, transparent sharing, and so forth.), how to facilitate a cell group, and characteristics of godly disciple-makers. I like to teach this manual in a home setting to provide a small group feeling and give the group opportunity to practice small group dynamics. This manual should include teaching about the ideal order of a cell meeting (e.g., the 4 Ws: Welcome, Worship, Word, and Works).

DISCIPLESHIP CONTINUUM

The process of maturing and becoming like Jesus lasts a lifetime. The goal of the Christian life is to continue to grow and become like Jesus until we are in heaven. Jesus, in Matthew 28:18-20, gives us a broad definition of what that might look like. He spent three years with his disciples, but they had many more lessons to learn after their three year stint. The Holy Spirit provided the disciples with many more growth experiences.

Several years ago I was coaching a pastor named Jim Corley in Tucson, Arizona whose church was in transition to become a cell church. Jim's church had already made it their mission to make disciples who make disciples—even before making the transition to become a cell church. My challenge as a coach was to connect cells with making disciples.

We prayed about how to do this and came up with a continuum of what the discipleship process might look like. You'll notice the interaction between discipleship within the cell and the completion of each stage of the equipping track. We envisioned the discipleship process in at least five stages, and we labeled those stages D1-5.

- D-1 disciple: personal growth in Jesus through devotions and relational building with those at the closest level. Learning how to walk in community with other members of a cell group, dealing with conflict, growing in love for others in spite of differences, and speaking directly with people rather than gossiping. Starting the equipping track and finishing the first manual on doctrine.
- D-2 disciple: learning how to use the gifts of the Spirit in the context of the group and helping others recognize their gifts and talents. Growing in the priesthood of all believers through taking active part in the life of the cell and being willing to help out in cell activities. Continuing church-wide equipping at the first level and finishing the manual on the inner life and how to have a quiet time.
- D-3 disciple: evangelizing with the group to those who don't know Jesus. Being willing to plan evangelistic activity with other group members and becoming fishers of men, like Jesus commanded. Continuing in the

church-wide equipping and finishing the manual on evangelism.

- D-4 disciple: preparing to form part of a team to start a new cell group. Participating on a higher level by leading the lesson and preparing to launch out into new territory. Finishing the manual on leading a small group.
- D-5 disciple: preparing to disciple new leadership through becoming a cell leader coach. Taking the second level equipping and supervising a new leadership team.

The D numbering doesn't have to stop with a D1-5 because we know that the process of discipleship transformation doesn't stop this side of heaven. Jim Corley, in fact, went beyond the D1-5 numbering and developed an equipping path that took people all the way to becoming a pastor. In the box below, you can see how pastor Corley modified this continuum to fit his own equipping material that changed over time.

Equipping Level I

1. Join a cell group.
2. Complete the course Crossfire (offered during Sunday school, in a Saturday seminar, or be fore/after cell).
- **Action step:** Get baptized and become a member.
3. Attend an encounter retreat.
- **Action step:** Break sinful habits.
4. Complete the course How to Have a Quiet Time (offered during Sunday school, in a Saturday seminar, or before/after cell).
- **Action steps:** Practice regular personal devotions, be assigned an accountability partner by the cell leader, agree to serve as an apprentice cell leader, complete the spiritual life assessment.

---

5. Complete the course How to Evangelize (offered during Sunday school, in a Saturday seminar, or before/after cell).
•   **Action step:** Evangelize and set a launch date for your own cell group.
6. Complete the course How to Lead a Cell Group (offered during Sunday school, in a Saturday seminar, or before/after cell).
•   **Action step**: Launch cell group.

Equipping Level II

1. Be leading an active cell group.
2. Complete the course How to Study the Bible for Yourself (offered during Sunday school, in a Saturday seminar, or online).
3. Complete the course How to Study the Bible for Sharing with Others (offered during Sunday school, in a Saturday seminar, or online).
4. Complete two of the following courses:
    • The Pentateuch
    • The Life of Christ
    • The Book of Acts
    • The Epistles

Action steps for Level II:
•   Multiply a cell group at least once.
•   Take a short-term missions trip.

Equipping Level III

•   Ministers Study Program (this is a self-study program that is guided by a mentor. It is offered through the Christian and Missionary Alliance, and the goal is for someone to become a licensed Christian worker).

Equipping Level IV
•   Year-long self-funded internship (requirement: completion of stages I–III)

FINDING THE RIGHT MATERIALS

Many leaders assume that the magical formula lies in finding just the right material, but the reality is that most cell churches pass through multiple revisions of their equipping material before finding the right fit. Initial failure often occurs because a church tries to copy another church's material in its entirety. As time passes, the church realizes that the equipping material doesn't fit its unique context and identity.

Specific Material

There are two major points to remember when selecting equipping material for your cell church. First, is it biblical? Does it reflect the pure doctrine "once delivered by the saints"? Second, is it connected with your cell church philosophy? In other words, is the equipping conducive to convert every member into a disciple-maker?

Ralph Neighbour's equipping track offers a number of booklets. Neighbour has spent the major part of his life perfecting equipping material for every aspect of cell life—new Christian development, Bible curriculum, evangelism equipping, gifts of the Spirit, spiritual warfare, and more. [70] The believer is told from day one that eventually he or she will participate in forming part of a new group.

A famous cell church in South Africa called Little Falls Christian Centre developed its own material based on Ralph Neighbour's equipping series. They asked for permission to synthesize Ralph Neighbour's material, and it only takes four months to complete, rather than the length of one year. LFCC's equipping starts with basic doctrinal equipping in *Welcome to Your New Family;* then the new believer receives more in-depth discipleship in the *Arrival Kit Companion*; the *Reaching the Lost* booklet prepares the potential leader to evangelize, whereas the Cell Leader Equipping Manual launches him into cell leadership. A more in-depth manual, taught in a retreat, accompanies each booklet.

I've developed my own nine-month equipping track that takes a person from conversion all the way to facilitating a small group, or being part of a team. Each book in my discipleship equipping contains eight lessons. Each lesson has interactive activities that help the trainee reflect on the lesson in a personal, practical way. The person being trained should also participate in a small group in order to experience community while learning about it. In a nutshell, the equipping includes:

- An interactive book on basic biblical truths called *Live*. This book covers key Christian doctrines, including baptism and the Lord's Supper.
- The next book is *Encounter*, which guides the believer to receive freedom from sinful bondages. The *Encounter* book can be used one-on-one or in a group.
- Then the trainee uses *Grow*, to learn the spiritual practice of daily devotional time. *Grow* gives step-by-step instruction for having a daily quiet time, so that the believer will be able to feed him or herself through spending daily time with God.
- Then the person studies *Share*, which helps him or her learn how to evangelize. This book instructs the believer how to communicate the gospel message in an appealing, personal way. This book also has two chapters on small group evangelism.
- The fifth book is called *Lead*. This book prepares the person to launch a cell, or be part of a leadership team.

I also have developed a second-level equipping for those who have completed the first level. [71]

The material used in most traditional churches is endless. It is often great material, but it doesn't lead to a specific destination. Because the focus is on general education, there's no limit to what must be learned and no direction for the person being educated.

Materials from Cell Churches World Wide

Most cell churches around the world have developed their own materials. You can take advantage of their experiences. Someone has said that plagiarism is copying one person's material while research is gathering the materials of many. On a more serious note, plagiarism is a sin and the law forbids us to make whole photocopies of someone else's copyrighted material. We can, however, use their ideas and synthesize them with our own.

The Christian Center in Guayaquil, Ecuador borrowed concepts from Neighbour, the Elim Church, and the International Charismatic Mission. Little Falls Christian Centre took the best from Neighbour and then synthesized it into four booklets and manuals. [72] I recommend the following process:

1. Obtain copies of other equipping material: Research what is out there. Obtain copies of the material from cell churches you respect. [73]
2. Test the material: After receiving materials from a variety of sources, review and test them to determine those that best fit your church. Some material works better in more educated churches, while others are designed to equip those with less schooling. You will also want to evaluate the stance taken on specific theological issues to make sure they line up with the beliefs of your church.

3. Listen to God and adapt: Most importantly, listen to God. Discover what's best for your own particular church and context. You'll want to include in your materials your specific doctrinal slant. God has been uniquely working in your own situation. Adapt the materials according to your own needs.

Create Your Own Materials

Over time, most cell churches establish their own materials. It's just more comfortable and it fits better. God has made your church unique, with particular convictions and methodology. You'll want to reflect this uniqueness in your material.

ENVISIONING FUTURE DISCIPLES

I was with one church in Brazil where the pastor asked me how to set goals for cell multiplication. I told him that the place to start in goal setting is the equipping path. In other words, cell churches don't allow a person to form part of a new cell team unless he or she has completed the entire discipleship-equipping path and is actively involved in a cell group. This means that the goal of the church is to first get people through the equipping. The discipleship-equipping path allows a church to know how to chart the future. If no one is in the equipping, very few multiplication possibilities exist. A church needs to have a workable discipleship equipping in place to make this practical.

Other churches are not ready to set goals for new disciples because new people are not coming to the church and thus, no one is going through the equipping. Another scenario is when the pastor is still learning about cell church. I've coached some pastors who don't really understand the cell vision. My job as coach is to help them understand the values behind cell ministry, how to do cell ministry, and their own role in the process. In these situations, it doesn't help to set goals until the pastor has embraced the values that will propel him to keep pressing on in the in the process of making disciples who make disciples.

A pastor can plaster goals on the wall and include them in the bulletin, but if the true vision and values are not maintained, people become weary and drop out. When this happens, the church will become critical and disillusioned and often will go back to previous programs or say, "Cell church simply doesn't work."

While there are pitfalls to goal setting, I do think it's important for pastors to move ahead in a specific direction. And when I'm coaching pastors, I try to help them discern a healthy goal for making disciples who make disciples—something that will help them move forward without discouraging them. When we determine a healthy goal for the year, I then coach the pastor and the church each week according to those goals and dreams. Normally unexpected obstacles crop up and often a pastor has to change the goal midstream to adjust to reality. Yet, the fact that a pastor is envisioning a brighter future is important.

Juan and Paola Paniagua are lead pastors of a Nazarene Church in Stamford, Connecticut. They started with four cell groups in 2011 and by 2012 had achieved the goal of twenty-two cell groups. Each month we looked at those who would graduate from the discipleship equipping, the health of each group, unforeseen obstacles, and what kind of coaching each group received. Summer was especially difficult for the church because the members scattered in the summer and leadership commitment went way down. It was hard for them to reignite the troops and get them ready for the fall.

Yet, their goal for making new disciples gave them a new freedom and brought a lot of past cell knowledge into sharp focus. They met their goal, yet it took every ounce of effort and a lot of congregational work to reach it. I told them that 2013 would be a year of mending the nets, focusing on the health of the cells, the community within the groups, celebrating the leaders accomplishments, and preparing each group spiritually for 2014.

Just like there are seasons of life, I've discovered there are seasons for small group development. It doesn't always work on a one year regimented multiplication pattern. A lot of factors must be taken into account.

GET STARTED

The journey of a thousand miles begins with the first step. Take that step today, whether that means fine-tuning your existing discipleship equipping path or ordering the materials for the one you're creating. Remember that many more steps will be required as you perfect your equipping path. If you keep at it, you'll discover that the secret to a great discipleship equipping path is continual testing and perfecting until the equipping actually does what it's supposed to do: produce more and better disciples who are also making disciples.

Chapter Nine

DISCIPLESHIP THROUGH COACHING

Logic says that Jesus should have spent the vast majority of his time concentrating on the multitude. After all, he was only going to be on earth for a short time, and the masses had so many needs. Yet of the five hundred fifty verses in Mark that record Christ's ministry, two hundred eighty-two show Jesus relating to the public, while two hundred sixty-eight illustrate his working with the twelve. [74] Why would Jesus spend so much time with so few disciples? Even within the group of twelve, he gave more attention to James, Peter, and John. Jesus knew he needed to focus on the few in order to prepare those who would actually lead the multitude. The strategy worked. Acts 2:41-42 says: "Those who accepted his [Peter's] message were baptized, and about three thousand were added to their number that day. They devoted themselves to the apostles' teaching and to the fellowship, to the breaking of bread and to prayer."

Many pastors forget this principle. Unlike Jesus, they concentrate on the multitude and don't develop disciple-makers. Some pastors spend most of their time preparing their sermon to those hearers who come on Sunday. The problem is that disciples are not primarily formed through hearing a message. Other pastors prioritize counseling those who come through the church doors. Counseling, like preaching, is important. The problem is dependency and ministry extension. In fact, the two are connected. Because the pastor creates a dependency on himself, he is not able to reach more people.

The only way for a pastor to go beyond himself is to follow the pattern of Jesus: concentrate on the disciple-makers who will then pastor the multitude. Why? Because they will provide care for the rest of the church.

This was the same principle Jethro communicated to Moses after seeing him serving as judge from morning until evening (Exodus 18:13). Jethro said to Moses, "You and these people who come to you will only wear yourselves out. The work is too heavy for you; you cannot handle it alone" (Exodus 18:18). Moses needed to concentrate on the leaders who would then care for leaders until each member in a group of ten would be pastored.

Although the word *coaching* is not used in Exodus, the principle is the same. It's discipling the disciple-makers. This is what Jesus did also when he concentrated on the twelve who then coached the key leaders of the early church. The essence of coaching is discipling a few who in turn minister to others. Coaching in the cell church ensures that those who are discipling others are also receiving discipleship. Effective cell coaches zero in on the particular needs of each leader through listening, teaching, encouragement, and strategizing. Effective coaches care for the person's spiritual, emotional, familial, and personal needs.

The word *coach* is descriptive of the role a person plays as he or she supports cell facilitators under his or her care. It is not a sacred term. In fact, churches use many terms to identify the role played by the cell group coach: supervisor, section leader, G12 leader, cell overseer, cell sponsor, even L (which is the Roman numeral for 50). I've written extensively in other books about the different coaching structures that cell churches use.[3]

KEYS TO DISCIPLE LEADERS THROUGH COACHING

In a church plant or smaller church, the lead pastor does the lion's share of the coaching. In fact, coaching the cell facilitators should be the main role of the lead pastor. He needs to do what it takes to ensure the cell group leaders are healthy spiritually, prioritizing their families, and leading the cell group teams effectively. In larger cell churches with numerous cell groups, the lead pastor will focus on those who are coaching other cell team leaders (Jethro principle).

The number of cell group leaders a coach should oversee varies from church to church, depending upon the vision of the church and the capacity of the coach. If the coach also leads a small group, I would say that the coach should not take on more than three leaders. If the coach doesn't lead a small group, five is acceptable. When coaches care for more than five people, the quality often suffers.

---

4 In my book, *Passion and Persistence: How the Elim Church's Cell Groups Penetrated an Entire City for Jesus* (Houston, TX: Touch Publications), I talk about Elim's coaching structure, how their coaches are organized, what each level of coach does, the schedules, and how coaches are developed. I have two books on the G12 structure: Groups of Twelve (Houston, TX: Touch Publications, 1999) and From Twelve to Three (Houston, TX: Touch Publications, 2002). These book explain how G12 groups are organized and how they can be adapted.

I encourage mother cell leaders to coach the daughter cell leaders from their own group, if the mother cell leader is willing. The reason is because a relationship already exists between mother and daughter leader. Like a mother caring for her children, the mother cell leader has a special affinity for the new team leader and will most likely take greater care in visiting and ensuring his or her success. However, sometimes the mother leader is not able to coach the daughter cell leader because of time constraints, desire, or coaching ability. In these cases, it's best to assign a coach to the new team leader. The key is that each new leader has a coach who is praying, visiting, and serving the leader.

The best coaches have led and ideally multiplied cell groups. They are in the battle and have come from the cell system. Yet, not all leaders are great coaches. It's like basketball, football, or any sport. The best players are not necessarily the best coaches and the best coaches possibly were mediocre players, because playing and coaching requires different skill sets.

I recommend at least once per month coaching meetings in a group context (the coach with all of those leaders he or she is coaching) and once per month one-on-one between leader and coach. The group context brings out common problems and encourages the leaders to interact with one another. Individual coaching helps the coach meet the deep personal needs with each leader (e.g., family, personal needs, job, and spiritual life).

Some leaders need to meet more frequently than two times per month. Other leaders need less time. Jim Egli, who did his Ph.D. on cell ministry, writes,

> Coaches need a personal meeting with their small group director or pastor at least monthly. Small group leaders need two connections with their coach each month—one that focuses on ministry to them personally and one that

focuses on the mission of their group.... At bare minimum coaches should meet with their leaders at least once a month. The big advantage of meeting twice a month or every other week is that it enables you to move beyond personal ministry to your small group leaders to actual planning and problem-solving. [75]

I've seen some cell churches overextend their coaches with too many coaching meetings. This might work well for a particular time period, but in the long haul, burnout can ensue. I think it's essential to be balanced with regard to the number of coaching meetings.

One of the foundational ways of coaching is visiting the cell leader's group. In this way the coach can see what's really happening—not just what the leader says is taking place. When the coach does visit the cell, I encourage him or her to blend in as one of the cell members and to participate like any other member in the cell group.

Visiting a cell group is one of the best ways for the coach to observe cell leader patterns. Does the team leader talk too much? Not enough? How does the leader deal with the talkers? The silent ones? Did he or she follow the cell lesson plan? End on time? When talking with the leader personally about the cell, start with positive aspects and then highlight areas that need to improve. This will help in the discipleship process and encourage the leader to grow closer to Jesus.

HOW TO DISCIPLE LEADERS THROUGH COACHING

Andre Agassi, the famous tennis player, wrote his personal memoir entitled, Open. Agassi describes some terrible coaching experiences, but the one coach he extols is a man named Gil.

Why did Agassi feel Gil was such a great coach? Because Gil adapted his coaching to meet Agassi's needs. Former coaches gave Agassi general exercises. Gil studied Agassi's specific needs and adjusted the coaching regimen accordingly. Gil even built a gym in Agassi's garage and crafted all the exercise machines with Agassi in mind. He prepared specific exercises for Agassi, knowing his specific game and needs. In the following years, Agaasi went on to win all four grand slam tournaments, and Agassi attributes much of his success to Gil, his coach.

Effective coaches hone in on the specific needs of the players. What is the leader lacking? What particular needs does the leader have? There are specific disciplines that effective coaches practice in the process of discipling the leaders under their care.

Discipling through Prayer

Effective coaches cover their leaders in prayer, knowing that God gives the victory and answers prayer. Paul said to the Colossian house church, "For though I am absent from you in body, I am present with you in spirit and delight to see how orderly you are and how firm your faith in Christ is" (Colossians 2:15). Even though Paul wasn't physically present with the church, he was there in spirit. It's possible to be present spiritually with the leader through prayer. The Trinity is the best coach and loves to respond to believing prayer.

Coaches go to battle on behalf of the leaders under their care and provide spiritual protection against Satan's onslaughts. Effective coaches cover the leaders with a prayer shield and then when they talk personally, there is a unity that has already been developed through prayer. [76] I encourage coaches to pray continually for their leaders, and then tell them about those prayers. This will help tremendously in the spiritual realm, but this fact will also give the leaders renewed hope and confidence in the ministry.

Discipling through Listening

Often the coach feels inadequate to coach because he feels he doesn't know enough. Yet, I often tell them that the most important element is a listening ear. Often the leader already knows what to do. Coaches can get so focused on what they want to say that they forget that the real work is listening.

The coach needs to recognize that his or her agenda is secondary to the leader's agenda. A great coach knows when to shut up and let the other person speak. The human mind processes ideas and thoughts far faster than a person can speak them (by five to one), so it's easy to drift or daydream when someone is talking. The coach must concentrate to effectively listen, and it's not easy.

Preparing to listen requires some pre-meeting homework. Such preparation involves thinking about each leader's circumstances and needs. It's a great idea to write down notes and insights about the leader that can be reviewed before the next meeting. This helps the coach remember past conversations and prepares the coach to listen more intently.

Great coaches don't just listen to what has taken place in the cell but are also concerned about the leader's heart and life in general—marriage, emotional struggles, children, devotional life, and work. Often there are burdens that need to be shared in order for the leader to do a better job. The coach draws the leader out through careful listening.

Discipling through Encouragement

Barnabas is known as the "son of encouragement." He encouraged Paul and through his encouragement he helped Paul become an effective disciple of Jesus Christ. He saw beyond the rough edges, personally approached Paul, and then accompanied Paul on his journeys.

Why is encouragement so important? Because small group team leaders often don't feel they are doing a great job. They compare themselves with others, and they feel like a failure. They hear about the other team leader who already multiplied his cell and won multiple people to Jesus. The leader can easily suffer from feelings of inadequacy. "Why aren't more people coming to my cell group?" he wonders. Effective coaches use every opportunity to encourage the leader. "Jim, you show up for every cell group. Great job. That takes a lot of effort because I know you are busy."

Although the small group leader is doing his or her ministry for Jesus, when the coach can be God's instrument of encouragement, it's God directly saying to the leader, "I appreciate you; keep on pressing on; your reward is in heaven."

Discipling through Caring

The pastor cares for the coach and the coach cares for the leaders. The leader in turn cares for the members. Everyone needs to be coached and cared for. Coaching helps the system to flow together—just like the early church.

Often the best way to care for the leader is to be a friend. Many people overlook this simple, yet powerful, principle, but I believe that is one of the keys to successfully coaching small group leaders. Jesus, the ultimate coach, revealed this simple principle in John 15:15 when he said to his disciples, "I no longer call you servants, because a servant does not know his master's business. Instead, I have called you friends, for everything that I learned from my Father I have made known to you."

Jesus entered into friendship with twelve sinful human beings, whom he mentored for three years. He ate with them, slept with them, and answered all their questions. The Gospel writer Mark describes the calling of the twelve this way: "He appointed twelve—designating them apostles—that they might be with him. . ." (Mark 3:14). Jesus prioritized *being with them* over a set of rules or techniques, and this is what caring is all about.

God doesn't want lone rangers. He wants us to practice the one-anothers at every level. And the coach can minister to those leaders under his or her care by simple love and friendship.

Discipling through Developing

Coaches develop the leaders in both formal and informal ways. A coach supports each leader's ministry by connecting them to necessary resources, such as curriculum, equipping, or prayer support.

You might want to go over a book with your leader or at least recommend one. Great resources will help your cell leaders strategize better. You might say, "John, here's a link to an article about listening. Please check it out and we'll go over this next time we meet." Or if John is not the type that would go to the internet to check it out, the coach would simply print it out and give it to the leader. Later the coach would ask the leader what he or she thought. If the leader is not willing to commit to doing it on his or her own, it might be a good idea to read the entire article with the leader.

Become a resource person, and you will improve yourself and the leaders under your care. A coach can contact the leaders online, sending them articles, quotes and encouragement through email. Communicating with your leaders online is a fast, quick, and effective way to provide resources. You can send instant prayer requests, real-time updates on cell ministry, and helpful material that will encourage them to press on in discouraging times. Information sent via email is great because your leaders can process the information privately while having it handy for the future.

Discipling through Strategic Planning

When we were missionaries in Ecuador having our first baby, Sarah, we were nervous. A midwife from the U.S. embassy helped greatly. She was cheerful, confident, and encouraging. She was right there in the hospital when our firstborn came into this world.

Coaches can help cell leaders tremendously through the birth process. They help the cell leader envision future disciple-makers by encouraging the leader to develop strategic planning to get everyone participating in the group. The coach might say, "Tony, have you noticed Jill in your group?" "Why don't you consider her as a future leader?"

The coach also reminds the cell leader that his strategic planning should include encouragement of all members to take the discipleship equipping, knowing that no one will be a future team member without graduating from the equipping process. Effective coaches also help in the birthing process as the group sends out a new team of leaders.

Discipling through Challenging

When a team leader is stagnant, the members feel it. They wonder what's wrong with the group. Vitality is lacking, the lesson is unprepared, and the leader exudes a certain dullness. Effective cell coaches are close enough to detect the leader's lifelessness. The coach must be willing to speak directly to the leader, knowing that the leader's negative spiritual condition will affect those in the group.

Paul, in his message to the Ephesian house church, said, "Instead, speaking the truth in love, we will in all things grow up into him who is the head, that is, Christ" (Ephesians 4:15). Great coaches seek to model this challenge for action by honest interaction and asking the hard questions. I encourage coaches to start with the phrase, "Can I have permission to share something with you." The leader should know that the coach will give a *straight answer* and not *beat around the bush*.

Yet, because the coach wants the best for the leader, the coach sprinkles a healthy dose of love in the mix. It's a good practice not to give correction until giving truthful and positive praises. And there's always something positive to observe and highlight. The positive encouragement will allow the leader to receive the challenge for correction.

COACHING IS MOST IMPORTANT

I often recommend Jim Egli and Dwight Marble's book, *Small Groups, Big Impact*. The authors conducted their research among three thousand small group leaders in twenty countries and wanted to know why some groups grow and why some cell churches do a better job than others. They discovered that growing small group-based churches prioritize prayer, practice pro-active coaching, and establish a culture of multiplication.

Yet, when all three of these activities were analyzed together, coaching was the key factor.

Jim Egli writes, "Of all the questions on the survey, one emerged as most important. That question asks small group leaders: 'My coach or pastor meets with me to personally encourage me as a leader.' Leaders that respond with 'often' or 'very often,' have groups that are stronger in every health and growth measure!" [77]

Most churches fail because they don't see coaching as critical. They don't prioritize coaching in their budget, nor do they take time to learn how to coach. They might even downplay the significance of coaching in their rush to start new groups. The research of Egli and Marble remind us that a healthy system of coaching keeps the cell church healthy and moving forward. Healthy cell churches disciple the disciple-makers.

THE CALL TO DISCIPLE-MAKING

I watched an extraordinary documentary called *Azorian: The Raising of the K-129*. The Azorian project was the secret attempt by the U.S. in 1974 to recover the sunken Soviet submarine K-129 from the bottom of the ocean. They almost pulled it off but the large mechanical claw or "capture vehicle" was unable to sustain the weight of the submarine and two-thirds of the K-129 sank back to the ocean floor. Some believe the mechanical claws failed to work properly because of the wrong choice of steel.

Unless our foundation is strong enough, it won't stand the test of time. Attendance growth, cell church growth, packaged models or even leadership development may become examples of faulty steel that does not deliver over time. Christ's call to make disciples is the biblical reason to implement cell ministry. Christ's call to make disciples who make disciples provides a sturdy foundation for cell ministry.

Jesus chose to minister and mold his disciples in a group, and we need to return to this form of discipleship today. God is calling his Church to make disciples in an atmosphere where community, participation, group evangelism, and multiplication flourish. The early Church thrived in a small house church environment where these elements were plentiful and disciples multiplied. The small house churches were connected to each other to further the discipleship process.

Throughout this book, we've looked at the cell church as an excellent, biblical way to make disciples who make disciples. The cell has a special function in molding disciples of Jesus Christ and so does the cell church system. Both are important in the process of making disciples who make disciples.

Now it's your turn. What will you do with the information you have learned? How will you apply it? Will you allow it to drive you to the next step in furthering Christ's mandate to make disciples of all nations? At the end of his life, Paul exhorted his own disciple, Timothy, "And the things you have heard me say in the presence of many witnesses entrust to reliable men who will also be qualified to teach others" (2 Timothy 2:2). The work of passing the baton to successive generations of disciple-makers must not stop due to a bad link in the chain. The discipleship process must continue until the trumpet sounds and Jesus comes back to reunite with a victorious Church that is producing disciples who make disciples.

FINAL NOTES

1. I have written one of those "all-purpose" books called *Reap the Harvest*. While they do serve an important purpose to give a birds-eye view of cell ministry, they only cover each theme lightly, in a general way.

2. Sinek, Simon (2009-09-23). *Start with Why: How Great Leaders Inspire Everyone to Take Action* (p. 29). Penguin Group US. Kindle edition.

3. Sinek, Simon (2009-09-23). *Start with Why: How Great Leaders Inspire Everyone to Take Action* (pp. 65-66). Penguin Group US. Kindle edition..

4. Sinek, Simon (2009-09-23). *Start with Why: How Great Leaders Inspire Everyone to Take Action* (p. 39). Penguin Group US. Kindle edition.

5. Michael J. Wilkins, *Following the Master* (Grand Rapids, MI: Zondervan, 1992), p. 109.

6. John Eldredge, *Waking the Dead* (Nashville, TN: Thomas Nelson, 2003), p. 197.

7. Robert Coleman, *The Master Plan of Evangelism* (Old Tappan, NJ: Revell, 1971), p. 33.

8. Yoido Full Gospel Church, like other churches in Korea, counts a person as a "member" if that person gives financially to the church, and thus there are more "members" than attendees.

9. César Castellanos preached that the twelve stones that Elijah used to build Jehovah's sacrifice were the key to God answering his prayer (Claudia and César Castellanos, audio cassette, *Como influir en otros [How to Influence Others]* January 2002, conference in Bogota). Castellanos says, "The model of the twelve restores the altar of God that is in ruins" (César Castellanos, *The Ladder of Success* [London: Dovewell Publications, 2001], p. 25). We're told that Elijah would not have chosen Elisha if Elisha would have been plowing with eleven instead of twelve oxen, and that the Holy Spirit at Pentecost came when Matthias had replaced Judas, thus completing the number twelve (Claudia and César Castellanos, The Vision of Multiplication, audio cassette [Bethany World Prayer Center: International Cell Conference, 2001]. César Castellanos and the pastors at ICM will tell you that the vision of the number twelve came directly from God, and therefore we must follow this revelation. They often justify this particular number by referring to a direct revelation from God..

10. When I use the word *celebration* in this book, I'm referring to the large group gathering to worship and hear God's word. Most celebration services take place on Sunday, but some churches have their large group gatherings on different days of the week.

11. In the Greek world, philosophers were surrounded by their pupils. The Jews claimed to be disciples of Moses (John 9:28) and the followers of John the Baptist were known as his disciples (Mark 2:18; John 1:35).

12. Michael J. Wilkins, *Following the Master* (Grand Rapids, MI: Zondervan, 1992), p. 279.).

13. Kevin Giles, *What on Earth Is the Church? An Exploration in New Testament Theology* (Downers Grove, IL: InterVarsity Press, 1995), p. 20.

14. David Watson, *Called and Committed* (Wheaton, IL: Harold Shaw Publishers, 1982), p. 17.

15. Joseph Hellerman, *When the Church Was a Family* (Nashville, TN: B&H

Academic, 2009), p. 125.

16. C. Norman Kraus, *The Community of the Spirit* (Waterloo, OH: Herald Press, 1993), p. 33

17. John W. Ellas, *Small Groups & Established Churches: Challenge and Hope for the Future* (Houston, TX: Center for Church Growth), p.41.

18. Rodney Clapp, *A Peculiar People* (Downers Grove, IL: InterVarsity Press, 1996), p. 90.

19. There are some aspects of individualism that are very biblical: diligence, creativity, and the rule of the law, to name a few. Yet, individualism that stirs a person to separate from others—including one's own family—does not originate with the Trinity and the many biblical examples and must be critiqued and even avoided. Some cultures naturally practice forms of bribery. Business deals are based on who you know and the favors you show toward those people. Those cultures feel that a the rule of the law is far too impersonal and prefer a relational approach through bribery. Scripture critiques bribery and calls it wrong, so this aspect of culture needs to be corrected based on God's word.

20. Bruce J. Malina, "Collectivism in Mediterranean Culture," in *Understanding the Social World of the New Testament,* Dietmar Neufeld and Richard E. DeMaris, eds. (Milton Park, Abingdon, Oxon; New York, NY : Routledge, 2010), p. 18.

21. Bruce J. Malina, "Collectivism in Mediterranean Culture," in Understanding the Social World of the New Testament, Dietmar Neufeld and Richard E. DeMaris, eds. (Milton Park, Abingdon, Oxon; New York, NY : Routledge, 2010), p. 19. .

22. Eddie Gibbs, *In Name Only* (Wheaton, IL: Bridgepoint Books, 1994), p. 183.

23. C. Norman Kraus, *The Community of the Spirit* (Waterloo, OH: Herald Press, 1993), p. 43.

24. C. Norman Kraus, *The Authentic Witness* (Grand Rapids, MI: Eerdmans, 1979), p. 121.

25. As quoted in Michael J. Wilkins, Following the Master (Grand Rapids, MI: Zondervan, 1992), p. 244.

parts"greater than the sum of the parts."

26. C. Norman Kraus, *The Authentic Witness* (Grand Rapids, MI: Eerdmans, 1979), p. 121.

27. Tod E. Bolsinger, *It Takes a Church to Raise a Christian* (Grand apids, MI: Brazos Press, 2004), p. 71. .

28. Rodney Clapp, *A Peculiar People* (Downers Grove, IL: InterVarsity Press, 1996), p. 194.

29. Richard C. Meyers, *One Anothering, Volume 2* (Philadelphia, PA: Innisfree Press, 1999), p. 24.

30. Stephen A. Macchia, *Becoming a Healthy Disciple* (Grand Rapids, MI: Baker Books, 2004), p. 96.

31. As quoted in Randy Frazee, *The Connecting Church* (Grand Rapids, MI: Zondervan, 2001), p. 13.

32. David Watson, *Called and Committed* (Wheaton, IL: Harold Shaw Publishers, 1982), p. 30.

33. Dietrich Bonhoeffer, *Life Together:* A Discussion of Christian Fellowship (New York, NY: Harper & Row 1954), p. 23.

34. Bilezikian, Gilbert (2009-08-23). *Community 101 (*p. 54). Zondervan. Kindle edition.

35. Gerhard Lohfink, *Jesus and Community* (Philadelphia, PA: Fortress Press, 1982), p. 42.

36. David Jaramillo wrote these words on the Joel Comiskey Group blog on February 27, 2013 (www.joelcomiskeygroup.com/blog_2/).

37. Michael J. Wilkins, *Following the Master* (Grand Rapids, MI: Zondervan, 1992), p. 247.

38. Larry Crabb, *Connecting* (Nashville: Word Publishing, 1997), p. 31.

39. David Sheppard, *Built As a City: God and the Urban World Today* (London: Hodder and Stoughton, 1974), p. 127.

40. As quoted in Bruce L. Shelley, *The Church: God's People* (Wheaton, IL: Victor Books, 1978), p. 34.

41. Roland Allen, *Missionary Methods: St. Paul's or Ours?* (Grand Rapids, MI: Eerdmans, 1962), pp. 84-94.

42. Bill Hull, *The Disciple-Making Pastor* (Old Tappan, NJ: Fleming H.

Revell, 1988), p. 126.

43. Gilbert Bilezikian, *Community 101* (Grand Rapids, MI: Zondervan, 2009), p. 99.

44. Carolyn Osiek and David L. Balch, *Families in the New Testament World* (Louisville, KY: Westminster John Knox Press, 1997), p. 35.

45. Nigel Wright, *The Radical Kingdom* (Lottbridge Drove, Eastbourne, UK: Kingsway Publications, 1986), pp. 34-35.

46. Elton Trueblood, in Edward F. Murphy, *The Gifts of the Spirit and the Mission of the Church* (Pasadena, CA: Fuller Theological Seminary, 1972), p. 152.

47. Roland Allen, *Missionary Methods: St. Paul's or Ours?* (Grand Rapids, MI: Eerdmans, 1962), p. 91.

48. Roland Allen, *The Spontaneous Expansion of the Church: and the Causes Which Hinder It* (London: World Dominion Press, 1956), p. 17.

49. *Boundaries*, (Grand Rapids, MI: Zondervan, 1992), pp. 99–100.

50. Robert E. Logan, *Beyond Church Growth* (Grand Rapids, MI: Fleming H. Revell, 1989), p. 128.

51. George Ladd, *A Theology of the New Testament* (Grand Rapids, MI: Eerdmans, 1974), p. 545.

52. Robert Banks, *Paul's Idea of Community* (Peabody, MA: Hendrickson Publications, 1994), p. 148.

53. Arthur Patzia, *The Emergence of the Church: Context, Growth, Leadership & Worship* (Downers Grove, IL: InterVarsity, 2001), pp. 153-154.

54. Sadly, some present day teachers have over emphasized the five-fold ministry by teaching that every church (large or small) must identify all four or five offices and that without all of these leadership gifts functioning, the local church is doomed to failure. Some of these teachers also infer that only the ones who have an evangelist gift should be evangelizing; only the ones with a pastoral gift should shepherd the local church; and only those who have the gift of apostle should oversee church plants.

55. Various gift surveys include: Dr. Mel Carbonell's gift survey that features a gift inventory and the DiSC personality evaluation. Contact:

1-800-501-0490 or www.uniquelyyou.com (published by Uniquely You, Inc.); Alvin J. VanderGriend's gift survey (developed and published by the Christian Reformed Church, CRC Publications). Contact: 1-800-4-JUDSON; Paul Ford's gift survey (published by ChurchSmart Resources). Contact: 1-800-253-4276; Christian Schwarz's gift survey (published by ChurchSmart Resources). Contact: 1-800-253-4276.

56. EAs quoted in Paul Ford, *Unleash Your Church* (Pasadena, CA: Charles E. Fuller Institute, 1993), p. 49.

57. Dale Galloway, *The Small Group Book* (Grand Rapids, MI: Fleming H. Revell, 1995), p. 122.

58. John Mallison, *Growing Christians in Small Groups* (London: Scripture Union, 1989), p. 9.

59. Richard Peace, *Small Group Evangelism* (Pasadena, CA: Fuller Theological Seminary, 1996), p. 36.

60. In 1998 my first and bestselling book, *Home Cell Group Explosion,* hit the market. The book showcased my research on explosive cell group multiplication and the church growth that followed. I taught a lot about how cells multiplied but not much about cell health and making disciples through cell ministry.

61. Robert and Julia Banks, *The Church Comes Home: A New Base for Community and Mission* (Australia: Albatross Books, 1986), p. 39.

62. Michael Green, *Evangelism in the Early Church* (Grand Rapids, MI: Eermans, 2003), Kindle edition, p. 25.

63. Abe wrote this series of blogs on www.joelcomiskeygroup.com/blog_2 in January 2013.

64. Gehring, p. 25.

65. Bill Beckham, "Chapter 3: The Church with Two Wings," in Michael Green, editor, *Church Without Walls* (London: Paternoster Press, 2002), pp. 27-28. ,

66. Paul Benjamin quoted in Michael Mack, *The Synergy Church* (Grand Rapids, MI: Baker Books, 1996), p. 64.

67. Neal F. McBride, *How to Build a Small Groups Ministry* (Colorado Springs, CO: NavPress, 1995), p. 128.

68. Ralph Neighbour, Jr. "7 Barriers to Growth," Cell Church magazine, Summer, 1997: 16.

69. Mature leaders who have taken lots of equipping in the past could be given credit for subjects they've already mastered (e.g., Bible doctrine, evangelism, how to have a quiet time). However, I think it's a good idea to require that all members go through the second step (inner life development which usually includes an encounter-with-God retreat) and take the multiplication step (last step).

70. Touch materials can be purchased from TOUCH Outreach Ministries, 624 West 21st Street, Houston TX 77008, USA; Phone 713-861-6629; Fax: 713-861-6629; Email:sales@touchusa.org; http://www.touchusa.org. Their phone number to order books is 1-800-735-5865.

71. I have two other books (*Coach and Discover*) that are part of my advanced level equipping. The book *Discover* focuses on how a cell leader can discover his or her own spiritual gifts(s) and help others in the group find theirs. My book *Coach* helps a small group leader coach someone else who is leading a group.

72. Contact Little Falls Christian Centre at lfcc@iafrica.com. Their web site is: http://www.cellchurchint.co.za/ or http://www.lfcc.co.za/

73. For my own materials, see http://store.joelcomiskeygroup.com/allbobyjoco.html or by calling 951-567-3394. Touch materials (Ralph Neighbour) can be purchased from TOUCH Outreach Ministries, 624 West 21st Street, Houston TX 77008, USA; Phone 713-861-6629; Fax: 713-861-6629; email: sales@touchusa.org; http://www.touchusa.org. Their phone number to order books is 1-800-735-5865.

74. Jim Egli and Paul M. Zehr, *Alternative Models of Mennonite Pastoral Formation* (Elkhart, IN: Institute of Mennonite Studies, 1992), p. 43.

75. Jim Egli and Dwight Marble, *Small Groups, Big Impact* (Saint Charles, IL: Churchsmart Resources, 2011), p. 60.

76. God revolutionized our lives in 1995 after reading Peter Wagner's book *Prayer Shield* (Regal Books, 1992). Both Celyce and I realized that it wasn't enough to send out "prayer letters" to friends. We needed to have specific prayer partners. One of the best ways to coach leaders is to encourage the leaders to have a prayer shield (those who are praying for the leader) and to be part of the prayer shield for the leader.

77. Jim Egli and Dwight Marble, *Small Groups, Big Impact* (Saint Charles, IL: Churchsmart Resources, 2011), p. 57.

RESOURCES BY JOEL COMISKEY

Joel Comiskey's previous books cover the following topics

- Leading a cell group (*How to Lead a Great Cell Group Meeting*, 2001, 2009).
- How to multiply the cell group (*Home Cell Group Explosion*, 1998).
- How to prepare spiritually for cell ministry (*An Appointment with the King*, 2002, 2011).
- How to practically organize your cell system (*Reap the Harvest*, 1999; *Cell Church Explosion*, 2004).
- How to train future cell leaders (*Leadership Explosion*, 2001; *Live*, 2007; *Encounter*, 2007; *Grow*, 2007; *Share*, 2007; *Lead*, 2007; *Coach*, 2008; *Discover*, 2008).
- How to coach/care for cell leaders (*How to be a Great Cell Group Coach*, 2003; *Groups of Twelve*, 2000; *From Twelve to Three*, 2002).
- How the gifts of the Spirit work within the cell group (*The Spirit-filled Small Group*, 2005, 2009; *Discover*, 2008).
- How to fine tune your cell system (*Making Cell Groups Work Navigation Guide*, 2003).
- Principles from the second largest church in the world (*Passion and Persistence*, 2004).
- How cell church works in North America (*The Church that Multiplies*, 2007, 2009).
- How to plant a church (*Planting Churches that Reproduce*, 2009)
- How to be a relational disciple (*Relational Disciple*, 2010).
- How to distinguish truth from myths (*Myths and Truths of the Cell Church*, 2011).
- What the Biblical foundations for cell church are (*Biblical Foundations for the Cell-Based Church*, 2012).

**All of the books listed are available from Joel Comiskey Group
by calling toll-free 1-888-511-9995 or by ordering at:** 175
www.joelcomiskeygroup.com

How To Lead A Great Cell Group Meeting: So People Want to Come Back

Do people expectantly return to your group meetings every week? Do you have fun and experience joy during your meetings? Is everyone participating in discussion and ministry? You can lead a great cell group meeting, one that is life changing and dynamic. Most people don't realize that they can create a God-filled atmosphere because they don't know how. Now the secret is out. This guide will show you how to:

- Prepare yourself spiritually to hear God during the meeting
- Structure the meeting so it flows
- Spur people in the group to participate and share their lives openly
- Share your life with others in the group
- Create stimulating questions
- Listen effectively to discover what is transpiring in others' lives
- Encourage and edify group members
- Open the group to non-Christians
- See the details that create a warm atmosphere

By implementing these time-tested ideas, your group meetings will become the hot-item of your members' week. They will go home wanting more and return each week bringing new people with them. 140 pgs.

Home Cell Group Explosion: How Your Small Group Can Grow and Multiply

The book crystallizes the author's findings in some eighteen areas of research, based on a meticulous questionnaire that he submitted to cell church leaders in eight countries around the world, locations that he also visited personally for his research. The detailed notes in the back of the book offer the student of cell church growth a rich mine for further reading. The beauty of Comiskey's book is that he not only summarizes his survey results in a thoroughly convincing way but goes on to analyze in practical ways many of his survey results in separate chapters. The happy result is that any cell church leader, intern or member completing this quick read will have his priorities/values clearly aligned and ready to be followed-up. If you are a pastor or small group leader, you should devour this book! It will encourage you and give you simple, practical steps for dynamic small group life and growth. 175 pgs.

An Appointment with the King: *Ideas for Jump-Starting Your Devotional Life*

With full calendars and long lists of things to do, people often put on hold life's most important goal: building an intimate relationship with God. Often, believers wish to pursue the goal but are not sure how to do it. They feel frustrated or guilty when their attempts at personal devotions seem empty and unfruitful. With warm, encouraging writing, Joel Comiskey guides readers on how to set a daily appointment with the King and make it an exciting time they will look forward to. This book first answers the question "Where do I start?" with step-by-step instructions on how to spend time with God and practical ideas for experiencing him more fully. Second, it highlights the benefits of spending time with God, including joy, victory over sin, and spiritual guidance. The book will help Christians tap into God's resources on a daily basis, so that even in the midst of busyness they can walk with him in intimacy and abundance. 175 pgs.

Reap the Harvest: *How a Small Group System Can Grow Your Church*

Have you tried small groups and hit a brick wall? Have you wondered why your groups are not producing the fruit that was promised? Are you looking to make your small groups more effective? Cell-church specialist and pastor Dr. Joel Comiskey studied the world's most successful cell churches to determine why they grow. The key: They have embraced specific principles. Conversely, churches that do not embrace these same principles have problems with their groups and therefore do not grow. Cell churches are successful not because they have small groups but because they can support the groups. In this book, you will discover how these systems work. 236 pgs.

La Explosión de la Iglesia Celular: *Cómo Estructurar la Iglesia en Células Eficaces* (Editorial Clie, 2004)

This book is only available in Spanish and contains Joel Comiskey's research of eight of the world's largest cell churches, five of which reside in Latin America. It details how to make the transition from a traditional church to the cell church structure and many other valuable insights, including: the history of the cell church, how to organize your church to become a praying church, the most important principles of the cell church, and how to raise up an army of cell leaders. 236 pgs.

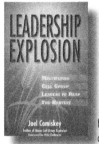

Leadership Explosion: *Multiplying Cell Group Leaders to Reap the Harvest*

Some have said that cell groups are leader breeders. Yet even the best cell groups often have a leadership shortage. This shortage impedes growth and much of the harvest goes untouched. Joel Comiskey has discovered why some churches are better at raising up new cell leaders than others. These churches do more than pray and hope for new leaders. They have an intentional strategy, a plan that will quickly equip as many new leaders as possible. In this book, you will discover the training models these churches use to multiply leaders. You will discover the underlying principles of these models so that you can apply them. 202 pgs.

FIVE-BOOK EQUIPPING SERIES

#1: Live   #2: Encounter   #3: Grow   #4: Share   #5: Lead

The five book equipping series is designed to train a new believer all the way to leading his or her own cell group. Each of the five books contains eight lessons. Each lesson has interactive activities that helps the trainee reflect on the lesson in a personal, practical way.

Live starts the training by covering key Christian doctrines, including baptism and the Lord's supper. 85 pgs.

Encounter guides the believer to receive freedom from sinful bondages. The Encounter book can be used one-on-one or in a group. 91 pgs.

Grow gives step-by-step instruction for having a daily quiet time, so that the believer will be able to feed him or herself through spending daily time with God. 87 pgs.

Share instructs the believer how to communicate the gospel message in a winsome, personal way. This book also has two chapters on small group evangelism. 91 pgs.

Lead prepares the Christian on how to facilitate an effective cell group. This book would be great for those who form part of a small group team. 91 pgs.

TWO-BOOK ADVANCED TRAINING SERIES

COACH   DISCOVER

Coach and Discover make-up the Advanced Training, prepared specifically to take a believer to the next level of maturity in Christ.

Coach prepares a believer to coach another cell leader. Those experienced in cell ministry often lack understanding on how to coach someone else. This book provides step-by-step instruction on how to coach a new cell leader from the first meeting all the way to giving birth to a new group. The book is divided into eight lessons, which are interactive and help the potential coach deal with real-life, practical coaching issues. 85 pgs.

Discover clarifies the twenty gifts of the Spirit mentioned in the New Testament. The second part shows the believer how to find and use his or her particular gift. This book is excellent to equip cell leaders to discover the giftedness of each member in the group. 91 pgs.

How to be a Great Cell Group Coach:
Practical insight for Supporting and Mentoring Cell Group Leaders

Research has proven that the greatest contributor to cell group success is the quality of coaching provided for cell group leaders. Many are serving in the position of a coach, but they don't fully understand what they are supposed to do in this position. Joel Comiskey has identified seven habits of great cell group coaches. These include: Receiving from God, Listening to the needs of the cell group leader, Encouraging the cell group leader, Caring for the multiple aspects of a leader's life, Developing the cell leader in various aspects of leadership, Strategizing with the cell leader to create a plan, Challenging the cell leader to grow.

Practical insights on how to develop these seven habits are outlined in section one. Section two addresses how to polish your skills as a coach with instructions on diagnosing problems in a cell group, how to lead coaching meetings, and what to do when visiting a cell group meeting. This book will prepare you to be a great cell group coach, one who mentors, supports, and guides cell group leaders into great ministry. 139 pgs.

Groups of Twelve: *A New Way to Mobilize Leaders and Multiply Groups in Your Church*

This book clears the confusion about the Groups of 12 model. Joel dug deeply into the International Charismatic Mission in Bogota, Colombia and other G12 churches to learn the simple principles that G12 has to offer your church. This book also contrasts the G12 model with the classic 5x5 and shows you what to do with this new model of ministry. Through onsite research, international case studies, and practical experience, Joel Comiskey outlines the G12 principles that your church can use today.

Billy Hornsby, director of the Association of Related Churches, says, "Joel Comiskey shares insights as a leader who has himself raised up numerous leaders. From how to recognize potential leaders to cell leader training to time-tested principles of leadership--this book has it all. The accurate comparisons of various training models make it a great resource for those who desire more leaders. Great book!" 182 pgs.

From Twelve To Three: *How to Apply G12 Principles in Your Church*

The concept of the Groups of 12 began in Bogota, Colombia, but now it is sweeping the globe. Joel Comiskey has spent years researching the G12 structure and the principles behind it.

From his experience as a pastor, trainer, and consultant, he has discovered that there are two ways to embrace the G12 concept: adopting the entire model or applying the principles that support the model.

This book focuses on the application of principles rather than adoption of the entire model. It outlines the principles and provides a modified application which Joel calls the G12.3. This approach presents a pattern that is adaptable to many different church contexts.

The concluding section illustrates how to implement the G12.3 in various kinds of churches, including church plants, small churches, large churches, and churches that already have cells. 178 pgs.

The Spirit-filled Small Group: *Leading Your Group to Experience the Spiritual Gifts.* The focus in many of today's small groups has shifted from Spirit-led transformation to just another teacher-student Bible study. But exercising every member's spiritual gifts is vital to the effectiveness of the group. With insight born of experience in more than twenty years of small group ministry, Joel Comiskey explains how leaders and participants alike can be supernaturally equipped to deal with real-life issues. Put these principles into practice and your small group will never be the same!

This book works well with Comiskey's training book, **Discover.** It fleshes out many of the principles in Comiskey's training book. Chuck Crismier, radio host, Viewpoint, writes, "Joel Comiskey has again provided the Body of Christ with an important tool to see God's Kingdom revealed in and through small groups." 191 pgs.

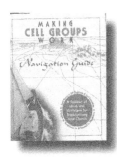

Making Cell Groups Work Navigation Guide: *A Toolbox of Ideas and Strategies for Transforming Your Church.* For the first time, experts in cell group ministry have come together to provide you with a 600 page reference tool like no other. When Ralph Neighbour, Bill Beckham, Joel Comiskey and Randall Neighbour compiled new articles and information under careful orchestration and in-depth understanding that Scott Boren brings to the table, it's as powerful as private consulting! Joel Comiskey has an entire book within this mammoth 600 page work. There are also four additional authors.

Passion and Persistence: *How the Elim Church's Cell Groups Penetrated an Entire City for Jesus*

This book describes how the Elim Church in San Salvador grew from a small group to 116,000 people in 10,000 cell groups. Comiskey takes the principles from Elim and applies them to churches in North America and all over the world. Ralph Neighbour says: "I believe this book will be remember as one of the most important ever written about a cell church movement! I experienced the *passion* when visiting Elim many years ago. Comiskey's report about Elim is not a *pattern* to be slavishly copied. It is a journey into grasping the true theology and methodology of the New Testament church. You'll discover how the Elim Church fans into flame their passion for Jesus and His Word, how they organize their cells to penetrate a city and world for Jesus, and how they persist until God brings the fruit." 158 pgs.

The Church that Multiplies: *Growing a Healthy Cell Church in North America*

Does the cell church strategy work in North America? We hear about exciting cell churches in Colombia and Korea, but where are the dynamic North American cell churches? This book not only declares that the cell church concept does work in North America but dedicates an entire chapter to examining North American churches that are successfully using the cell strategy to grow in quality and quantity. This book provides the latest statistical research about the North American church and explains why the cell church approach restores health and growth to the church today. More than anything else, this book will provide practical solutions for pastors and lay leaders to use in implementing cell-based ministry. 181 pgs.

Planting Churches that Reproduce: *Planting a Network of Simple Churchces*

What is the best way to plant churches in the 21st century? Comiskey believes that simple, reproducible church planting is most effective. The key is to plant churches that are simple enough to grow into a movement of churches. Comiskey has been gathering material for this book for the past fifteen Years. He has also planted three churches in a wide variety of settings. Planting Churches that Reproduce is the fruit of his research and personal experience. Comiskey uses the latest North American church planting statistics, but extends the illustrations to include worldwide church planting. More than anything else, this book will provide practical solutions for those planting churches today. Comiskey's book is a must-read book for all those interested in establishing Christ-honoring, multiplying churches. 176 pgs.

The Relational Disciple: *How God Uses Community to Shape Followers of Jesus*

Jesus lived with His disciples for three years and taught them life lessons as a group. After three years, he commanded them to "go and do likewise" (Matthew 28:18-20). Jesus discipled His followers through relationships—and He wants us to do the same. Scripture is full of exhortations to love and serve one another. This book will show you how. The isolation present in the western world is creating a hunger for community and the world is longing to see relational disciples in action. This book will encourage Christ-followers to allow God to use the natural relationships in life--family, friends, work relationships, cells, church, and missions to mold them into relational disciples.

You Can Coach: *How to Help Leaders Build Healthy Churches through Coaching*

We've entitled this book "You Can Coach" because we believe that coaching is more about passing on what you've lived and holding others accountable in the process. Coaching doesn't require a higher degree, special talent, unique personality, or a particular spiritual gift. We believe, in fact, that God wants coaching to become a movement. We long to see the day in which every pastor has a coach and in turn is coaching someone else. In this book, you'll hear three coaches who have successfully coached pastors for many years. They will share their history, dreams, principles, and what God is doing through coaching. Our hope is that you'll be both inspired and resourced to continue your own coaching ministry in the years to come.

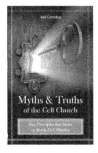

Myths & Truths of the Cell Church: *Key Principles that Make or Break Cell Ministry*

Most of the modern day cell church movement is dynamic, positive, and applicable. As is true in most endeavors, errors and false assumptions have also cropped up to destroy an otherwise healthy movement. Sometimes these false concepts caused the church to go astray completely. At other times, they led the pastor and church down a dead-end road of fruitless ministry. Regardless of how the myths were generated, they had a chilling effect on the church's ministry. In this book, Joel Comiskey tackles these errors and false assumptions, helping pastors and leaders to untangle the webs of legalism that has crept into the cell church movement. Joel then guides the readers to apply biblical, time-tested principles that will guide them into fruitful cell ministry. Each chapter begins with a unique twist. Well-known worldwide cell church leaders open each chapter by answering questions to the chapter's topic in the form of an email dialogue. Whether you're starting out for the first time in cell ministry or a seasoned veteran, this book will give you the tools to help your ministry stay fresh and fruitful.

Biblical Foundations for the Cell-Based Church

Why cell church? Is it because David Cho's church is a cell church and happens to be the largest church in the history of Christianity? Is it because cell church is the strategy that many "great" churches are using?

Ralph Neighbour repeatedly says, "Theology must breed methodology." Joel Comiskey has arrived at the same conclusion. Biblical truth is the only firm foundation for anything we do. Without a biblical base, we don't have a strong under-pinning upon which we can hang our ministry and philosophy. We can plod through most anything when we know that God is stirring us to behave biblically.

INDEX